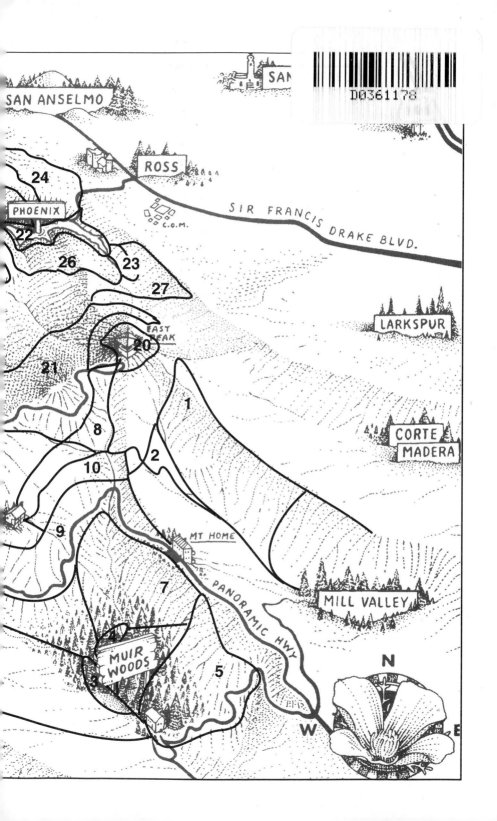

SAN ANSELMO

SAN

ROSS

24

PHOENIX

22

26   23

27

SIR FRANCIS DRAKE BLVD.

C.O.M.

LARKSPUR

EAST
PEAK

20

21

1

8

CORTE
MADERA

2

10

9

MT HOME

7

PANORAMIC HWY

MILL VALLEY

4

MUIR
WOODS

5

3

N

W   E

MT TAM

MT TAM

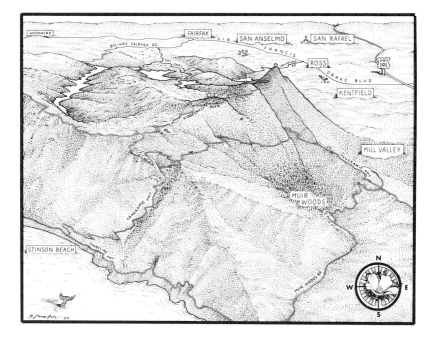

A Hiking, Running and Nature Guide

Don and Kay Martin
Illustrated by Bob Johnson

Second Edition

ISBN 0-9617044-4-6

Printed in the United States of America

Acknowledgments

We are extremely grateful to everyone who has helped and encouraged us in producing both editions of this book. We are especially thankful to Ron Angier, Greg Archbald, Marilyn Englander, Lincoln Fairley, Wilma Follette, Jim Furman, Dave Gould, Mary Johnson, Jim Locke, Eric Mohr, Brian Simon, Casey May, Al Molina, Eric McGuire, Candace McKinnon, Jerry Olmsted, Stephen Petterle,Tom Parker, Fred Sandrock, Bob Stewart, Meryl Sundove, Mia Monroe and the

California Native Plant Society
Golden Gate National Park Association
College of Marin Biology Department
Marin Municipal Water District
Marin Museum of the American Indian
Mt Tamalpais History Project
Mt Tamalpais State Park
Muir Woods National Monument
San Francisco State University Botany Department
and the public libraries and librarians of Marin County.

We would also like to thank our friends and hiking companions, Dick and Sharon Shlegeris, Bill and Dixie James, Ruth and Steve Nash, Shel and Joy Siewert, Phil and Mary Neff, Arlene Hansen, Mary Lou Grossberg, Sue Steele and especially Jennifer, Theresa, Susan and Greg Martin.

Although these people and organizations have provided valuable support, we are responsible for all errors that have occurred.

Picture Credits
9   Gravity Car: A.C. Graves-Ted Wurm Collection
13   Muir Woods Inn: Muir Woods National Monument
25   West Point Inn: photo by the authors
33   Dipsea Race: photo by the authors
45   Tamalpais Tavern: photo courtesy of Joseph A. Baird, Jr.
49   Phoenix Log Cabin: photo by the authors
71   Lake Lagunitas: photo by the authors
73   Giant Madrone Tree: photo by the authors
90   Old Railroad Ad: Ted Wurm Collection

Table of Contents

How to Use this Guide
Getting There and Finding Parking

Starting from Deer Park at 190'

Starting from Bon Tempe Lake at 660'

Starting from below Lake Lagunitas at 730'

Starting from Alpine Dam at 660'

Appendices

How to Use this Guide

Choosing A Hike or Outing

The two most important factors to consider when choosing a hike or run are distance and elevation change. If you are new to hiking, it's best to choose a hike conservatively. Three miles of hiking in rough terrain can take twice as long as three miles on flat terrain.

Once you've selected a range of distances and elevations, there are several questions you might consider. What is the best hike for this season? What wildflowers are in bloom? Where are the best view hikes? A good place to begin answering these questions is to look at the suggested hikes in Appendix A2, A3 and A4.

Hike Descriptions

If you're wondering how we arrived at the various ratings used in this book, here is a sample entry and brief description of the method used.

> *Distance:* 6.9 miles   Shaded: 60%
> *Elevation Change:* 1300'   Occasionally steep.
> *Rating:* Hiking - 10   Running - 7   Some bicycle traffic.
> *When to Go:* Excellent anytime, best from March to June.

Distance

Distance measurements were determined by a combination of methods including using information from other books and maps, and by pacing or timing hikes. Distances between points are accurate to about 0.1 miles, while overall distances are good to 0.2 miles.

Elevation Change

The elevation change was taken from other books and maps, and from USGS maps. For hikes that make one long trip up, then down, the elevation change is fairly accurate.

Hiking and Running Rating

The Hiking rating depends on aesthetics. How interesting is the hike? For example, the Simmons - Music Camp - Cataract Trails, Hike 17, has a variety of flora, rolling terrain and good views. We consider it interesting 90-100% of the time and so, rated it a 10. On the other hand, the Taylor - Concrete Pipe - Bullfrog Rd, Hike 30, travels mainly on roads and, in some areas, has little change in flora. We consider it interesting about 50-60% of the time and rated it a 6.

Obviously, this rating system is subjective and depends on what we like. Also, the rating system is dependent on the season. Our rating of hikes is based on the best possible conditions, the best season, views, weather and wildflowers.

The Running rating is based solely on footing conditions. If a trail has good footing conditions 90-100% of the time, we give it a 10. If the footing is good 80-90%, we rate it a 9. Stairs, rocky paths, exposed roots and steep slopes all reduce the running rating.

When To Go

The When to Go rating is based on flora and fauna, weather, season, views, trail and road conditions. Since winter provides rainfall and water runoff, while late winter and spring produce wildflowers, these two seasons are the best times to go on most hikes.

Using The Maps

The maps are based on USGS digital elevation data with data points 30 meters apart. However, the data has been smoothed, so that map resolution is about 100 meters. Both the top and bottom 3-dimensional maps show "3-D slices" cut from Mt Tamalpais, as shown in the figure below. The top map provides a perspective view while the bottom map is displayed so that no part of the map is any closer to the observer than any other part. Scales shown on the bottom map are not completely accurate since elevations have been exaggerated.

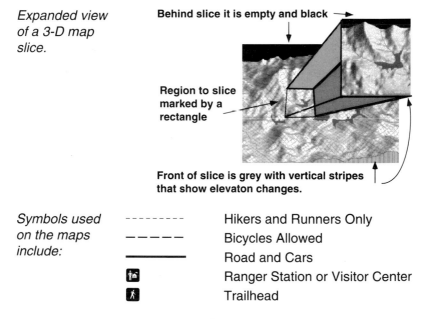

Expanded view of a 3-D map slice.

Behind slice it is empty and black →

Region to slice marked by a rectangle

Front of slice is grey with vertical stripes that show elevaton changes.

Symbols used on the maps include:

- - - - - - - - -   Hikers and Runners Only
— — — — —   Bicycles Allowed
——————   Road and Cars
🏠   Ranger Station or Visitor Center
🚶   Trailhead

Hikers, Runners and Bicyclists

The hikes in this book have been laid out to minimize contact between hikers and bicyclists. Where possible, hikes have been routed off bike roads and onto trails. Also, hikes that include roads for part of the trip usually head uphill, so that hikers can see bicyclists coming downhill. All bike roads are marked on the maps.

Precautions

Poison oak for some is a minor irritation, for most, a major irritation and for a few, a medical emergency. The best advice is to learn to identify the plant by its leaves and avoid touching it. An old saying is,

"Leaves of three, leave it be."

In fall, poison oak leaves turn crimson red and drop off. In winter, the bare branches are difficult to identify, yet still retain their toxic oils. It helps to stay on designated trails and to watch out for branches that lean out onto the trail or drape down

Poison Oak

over the path. Poison oak is very common on Mt Tamalpais.

Ticks and Lyme Disease

Ticks are also common on Mt Tamalpais and are especially noticeable during the rainy season from November to May. Recent field studies have shown that 1-2% of the western black-legged ticks in Marin County carry Lyme disease.

The best way to avoid ticks is to stay on trails. It also helps to wear light clothing so that ticks can be seen. Be sure to brush yourself frequently, especially after passing through tall grass or shrubs. After a hike, check yourself completely. Ticks anesthetize the skin before biting so you'll seldom feel the original bite.

Early removal of a tick reduces the risk of infection. Use tweezers rather than fingers. Grab the tick mouth parts as close to the skin as possible and pull straight out. Wash hands and clean the bite with an antiseptic.

Actual Size

Western Black-Legged Tick

The first recognizable symptom of Lyme disease is usually a ring-like red rash that occurs 3-30 days after the bite of an infected tick. The rash may grow to several inches in diameter, while clearing in the center, thus producing a ring. One or more rashes may occur and not always at the bite site. However, a rash only appears in 60-80% of infected persons. Other symptoms may include flu-like fever, chills, fatigue, headaches and a stiff neck. Since early diagnosis of Lyme disease is crucial, be sure to see a doctor if you think you have it.

Fluids

Fluids are essential when hiking or staying outdoors. Often, people go hiking or go to the beach and wind up the day with a mild headache. Usually, this is attributed to too much exposure, too much sun or too much wind. Many times, the problem is too little fluids. Hiking requires a minimum of 1/2 quart of fluids per hour, or more, depending on the temperature and elevation change. Alcohol does not count. It is a diuretic, which means that it removes fluid by osmosis in the stomach. It is always a good idea to carry water on a hike and to drink it regularly whether you feel thirsty or not.

Plan to drink at least 1/2 quart of fluid per hour on hikes.

Do not drink water from streams or lakes. It may contain giardia, a protozoa that can cause severe stomach problems until treated with antibiotics.

Fire

Wildfires are part of the natural history of Mt Tamalpais. As the Oakland hills fire has taught us, these wildfires can be deadly. During periods of extreme fire danger, both the state park and the water district lands may be closed.

Getting Lost

It is surprisingly easy to get lost on Mt Tamalpais, even when using an up-to-date book with good maps. There are four major reasons for this: there are lots of deer trails, a few trails are overgrown, some junctions lack signs, and people take short-cuts.

If you are in a new area, our advice is to follow the book carefully and note each junction on the map. Stay on trails and don't take shortcuts.

Disclaimer

Although we have tried to provide the best, most helpful information possible, there are omissions and errors. Also, nature is not static. Hillsides erode. Trails get rerouted. Trees fall down. Signs change and hikes change. In winter, some trails and roads may be impassable. This book is only a guide. We can not accept responsibility for trail conditions or for trail information. This is our disclaimer that we do not accept liability or legal responsibility for any injuries, damage, loss of direction or time allegedly caused by using this book. For the best information, check the local ranger stations.

Getting There and Finding Parking

Old Railroad Grade Trailhead in Mill Valley - Hikes 1, 2

From Highway 101, take the E. Blithedale exit to downtown Mill Valley, then take W. Blithedale to just past Lee St. The trailhead starts at a gate just as W. Blithedale crosses the creek. There is parking for about six cars here. More parking can be found in the half-mile before the trailhead.

Muir Woods - Hikes 3 to 6

From Highway 101, take the Shoreline Hwy (Hwy 1) turnoff, signed to Mt Tamalpais and Stinson Beach. Follow the Hwy 1 signs for three winding miles, then turn right on Panoramic Hwy.

After about one mile on Panoramic Hwy, take the dangerous Muir Woods turnoff to the left. At Muir Woods, parking is limited. Rangers prefer that hikers (in contrast to visitors) park in the lower annex parking lot farthest from the entrance.

Mtn Home Inn, Bootjack and Pantoll - Hikes 7 to 16

From Highway 101, take the Shoreline Hwy (Hwy 1) turnoff, signed to Mt Tamalpais and Stinson Beach. Follow the Hwy 1 signs for three miles, then turn right on Panoramic Hwy, which passes each of these areas in turn.

Parking at the Mtn Home Inn is difficult on Saturdays from 9-11 am when runners gather for a weekly run.

Parking at Bootjack and Pantoll costs $5.00 per day. There is a small free parking area for about 10 cars just past Pantoll on the Pantoll Rd. This is usually filled on weekends by 8:30 am. Parking can most easily be found at Bootjack.

Nearest bus: #63 stops at each location about four times a day on weekends only. Check the Golden Gate Transit schedules.

Rock Spring and East Peak - Hikes 17 to 21

From Highway 101, take the Shoreline Hwy (Hwy 1) turnoff, signed to Mt Tamalpais and Stinson Beach. Follow the Hwy 1 signs for three miles, then turn right on Panoramic Hwy. At Pantoll, turn right and head uphill on the Pantoll Rd to Rock Spring. Good parking.

To reach East Peak, turn right at Rock Spring on East Ridgecrest Blvd. Parking at East Peak costs $5.00.

Natalie Greene Park in Ross - Hikes 22 to 27

From Highway 101, take Sir Francis Drake Blvd west. In Ross, take Lagunitas Rd left to the park. There is parking for about 20 cars in the park and another 15 cars by the tennis club. Both of these areas fill quickly on weekend mornings. Do not park in "No Parking" areas.

Nearest bus: #20 stops every half hour at SFD and Lagunitas Rd.

Deer Park in Fairfax - Hikes 28, 29

From Highway 101, take Sir Francis Drake Blvd west through San Anselmo to Fairfax. Turn left on Pacheco (which is not marked), then right on Broadway, to pass in front of the Fairfax Theater. Just past the theater, turn left on the Bolinas-Fairfax Rd. Turn left on Porteous Ave and follow it as it winds around to Deer Park. There is parking for about 30 cars, but it can fill up with picnickers on weekends.

Nearest bus: Every half hour, #23 eastbound on SFD, westbound on Broadway, both stops near Bolinas Ave.

Bon Tempe Dam outside Fairfax - Hikes 30 to 32

From Highway 101, take Sir Francis Drake Blvd west through San Anselmo to Fairfax. Turn left on Pacheco (which is not marked), then right on Broadway, to pass in front of the Fairfax Theater. Just past the theater, turn left on the Bolinas-Fairfax Rd. Follow the road uphill for three miles, then turn left on Sky Oaks Rd and go up to the toll booth (pay fee). About 1/2 mile past the toll booth, turn right on the dirt road. There is limited parking below the dam with more parking down by Alpine Lake.

Nearest bus: #23 in Fairfax.

Lagunitas Lake outside Fairfax - Hikes 33 to 36

Same as Bon Tempe directions, only stay on the paved road from the toll booth all the way to the end. There is a Y-junction near the end of the road that is not well-marked. Take the right into the parking area which can hold lots of cars, but usually fills with picnickers on nice weekends. There is also an overflow parking area nearby.

Alpine Lake Dam outside Fairfax - Hike 37

From Highway 101, take Sir Francis Drake Blvd west through San Anselmo to Fairfax. Turn left on Pacheco (which is not marked), then right on Broadway, to pass in front of the Fairfax Theater. Just past the theater, turn left on Bolinas Avenue. Follow the Bolinas Rd for about eight winding miles. There is limited parking past the dam by the trailhead with more parking near the dam.

1 Blithedale Ridge - Corte Madera Trails

Distance: 4.2 miles   Shaded: 20%
Elevation Change: 1100'   One very steep section.
Rating: Hiking - 9   Running - 7   Heavy bicycle use on parts.
When to Go: Save this hike for cool, clear winter days.

Bring binoculars and camera for this roller-coaster hike that rolls along Blithedale Ridge offering stunning views of Mt Tam and Marin.

0.0 Start near the Old Railroad Grade trailhead located near the end of West Blithedale Ave. Go through the gate and head uphill on the dirt road. Stay to the right and watch for bicycles.

0.1 Junction. Turn right and take the H-Line FR as it starts a moderately steep climb out of the canyon and into open chaparral.

0.7 Two junctions #1. You can reduce the hill climbing by 300' and cut this hike short by a mile by heading left. Otherwise, go right on Blithedale Ridge to climb to a spectacular viewpoint of Mt Tamalpais.

1.2 Junction #2 with the Corte Madera Ridge FR. There are two great view spots near here. First, go left 50' for a great view down Warner Canyon and out towards San Francisco. Then return to this junction and continue on the road up to the next knoll.

1.3 Knoll and view spot. This picture-taking spot offers a striking profile of the East Peak of Mt Tamalpais. Return to jct #1.

1.9 Back at junction #1. Continue straight and up along the ridge.

2.8 Junction #3 with the Hoo-Koo-E-Koo FR. Note that there is both a trail and fire road called Hoo-Koo-E-Koo, which was reputedly named after a band of Miwok Indians that lived near the base of the mountain. It's worth continuing the climb another 100 yds up to Indian FR which offers panoramic views north.

2.8+ Indian FR. Great views of Bill Williams Canyon and points to the north. When ready to continue, backtrack 100 yds.

2.9 Junction. Take the Hoo-Koo-E-Koo FR right towards East Peak.

3.1 Two junctions #4. The Hoo-Koo-E-Koo trail heads left. Take the Corte Madera trail as it descends steeply alongside the creek. The trail crosses the creek four times, so if you lose the trail, look for it on the other side of the creek.

3.5 Junction with Horseshoe FR. Head right downhill.

3.6 Junction with the Old Railroad Grade. Continue left downhill.

4.2 Back at the trailhead.

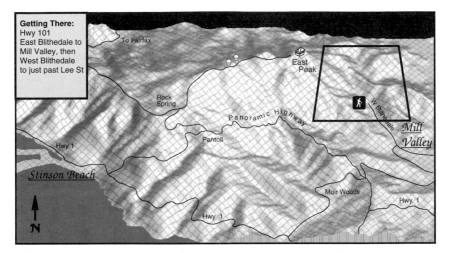

Getting There:
Hwy 101
East Blithedale to
Mill Valley, then
West Blithedale
to just past Lee St

To Fairfax

East
Peak

Rock
Spring

Panoramic Highway

Pantoll

W Blithedale

Mill
Valley

Stinson Beach

Hwy 1

Muir Woods

Hwy 1

Hwy 1

N

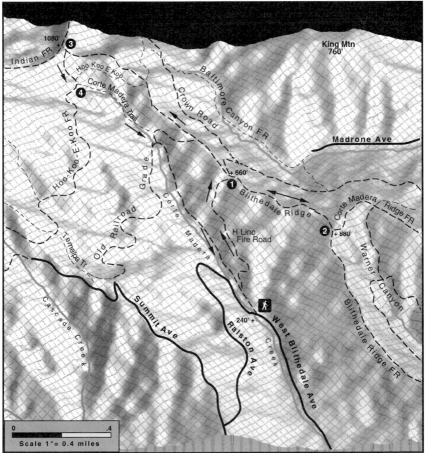

1080'

Indian FR

3

Hoo Koo E Koo

Corte Madera Trail

4

King Mtn
760'

Baltimore Canyon FR

Crown Road

Madrone Ave

Hoo-Koo-E-Koo FR

Old Railroad Grade

Corte Madera

+ 660'

1

Blithedale Ridge

Corte Madera Ridge FR

H Line
Fire Road

2

+ 880'

Warner Canyon

Tenelpa Tr

Cascade Creek

Summit Ave

Ralston Ave

240' +

West Blithedale Ave

Creek

Blithedale Ridge FR

0   .4

Scale 1" = 0.4 miles

8

2 Old Railroad Grade - Hoo-Koo-E-Koo

Distance: 7.4 miles   Shaded: 50%
Elevation Change: 1300'   Two steep downhill sections.
Rating: Hiking - 7   Running - 6   Heavy bicycle traffic.
When to Go: Best on cool, clear weekdays.

This hike follows the historic Old Railroad Grade as it gradually climbs up the mountain. Open chaparral areas provide great views.

0.0 Start at the Old Railroad Grade trailhead located near the end of West Blithedale Ave. Go through the gate and head uphill.

1.8 Junction #1 with Summit Ave and Fern Canyon Rd. The hike continues uphill on the paved road for 0.6 miles. Great views.

2.9 Two junctions and the Double Bowknot. Two roads separated by 100' head left and join to form Gravity Car Grade which leads to the Mtn Home Inn and Muir Woods.

Continue right to pass the concrete landing, Mesa Station, where passengers could transfer to gravity cars and coast down Gravity Car Grade. This road section is part of the famous Double Bowknot where tracks make a series of switchbacks and parallel each other five times. From 1896 to 1930, the Mt Tamalpais & Muir Woods Railway, better known as the "Crookedest Railroad in the World", attracted bay area residents and tourists to outings on the mountain.

3.2 Junction #2 with the Hoo-Koo-E-Koo FR. Continue left uphill.

Gravity Car

3.8 Junction #3. Head left, steeply down Hogback FR.

3.9 Junction. Take the signed Hoo-Koo-E-Koo trail left.

4.6 Junction. Take the Old Railroad Grade left for just 100 yds.

4.7 Back at junction #2. Leave the Old Railroad Grade and take the signed Hoo-Koo-E-Koo FR to the right. Watch for bicycles.

6.3 Two junctions #4. Take the Corte Madera trail as it descends steeply alongside the creek, which it crosses several times.

6.7 Junction with Horseshoe FR. Head right downhill.

6.8 Junction with the Old Railroad Grade. Continue left downhill.

7.4 Back at the trailhead.

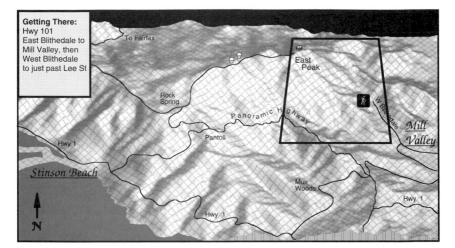

Getting There:
Hwy 101
East Blithedale to
Mill Valley, then
West Blithedale
to just past Lee St

To Fairfax

East
Peak

W Blithedale

Rock
Spring

Mill Valley

Panoramic Highway

Pantoll

Stinson Beach

Muir
Woods

Hwy 1

Hwy 1

Hwy 1

N

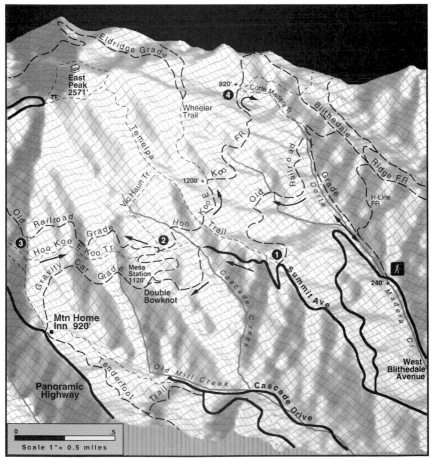

Eldridge Grade

East
Peak
2571'

920' +

Corte Madera Tr

Blithedale

Wheeler
Trail

❹

Temelpa Tr

FR

Ridge FR

Koo

1200' +

Koo E

Old

Railroad

Grade

Corte

H-Line
FR

Vic Haun Trf

Hoo

Trail

Old

Railroad

Grade

❸

Hoo Koo E Koo Tr

❷

❶

Summit Ave

240' +

Gravity

Car

Grade

Mesa
Station
1120'

Double
Bowknot

Cascade Creek

Madera Cr

**Mtn Home
Inn 920'**

West
Blithedale
Avenue

Tenderfoot

Trail

Old Mill Creek

Cascade Drive

**Panoramic
Highway**

0   5

Scale 1" = 0.5 miles

3 Muir Woods - Hillside Trails

Distance: 1.9 miles   Shaded: 100%
Elevation Change: 200'
Rating: Hiking - 10   Running - No, too crowded.
When to Go: Excellent anytime, best in spring for trillium.

This Muir Woods hike is the most heavily traveled trail on Mt Tam as it winds along the floor of a beautiful, virgin redwood forest.

0.0 Start at the Muir Woods parking lot. Follow the signed Main trail along the right side of Redwood Creek. The trail has several nature information signs describing the redwood forest. Also, you can pick up a brochure describing nature points along the way.

0.5 Cathedral Grove. A beautiful redwood grove dedicated to the founding of the United Nations in San Francisco in 1945. Tanoak and western swordfern are the dominant shrub-like growth under the redwood canopy, while redwood sorrel provides most of the ground cover. Ahead, the light green leaves of western azalea, hazel and big leaf maple stand out against the dark-green, redwood background.

0.7 Junction with Fern Creek. Continue left. Notice how some redwoods have an enormous number of sprouts growing out of the base, while others have a grey-green lichen growth on the bark.

0.9 Park boundary and junction #1. Bear left, cross the bridge and head up to Hillside Jct. Go left again and climb up the Hillside trail.

1.1 Ravine. The first of three small, picturesque ravines. Ferns, mosses, pink trillium, sorrel and the striking clintonia lie along the bank. Notice the large Douglas fir just past the streambed. Its bark differs from nearby redwoods in texture and in the moss covering. Redwoods often have lichens, but seldom mosses.

Trillium

1.6 Junction. The Hillside trail gently descends to the canyon floor. Stay right to enter Bohemian Grove with some of the tallest trees in the park, nearly 260'. Ahead at the bridge, look for spawning silver salmon and steelhead trout in wintertime.

1.8 Snack shop, gift shop and restroom facilities.

1.9 Parking lot. Continue walking along the creek to see several large red alders in a riparian setting. Further downstream, across from the highway entrance, notice the incredibly tangled buckeye trees with moss-covered trunks criss-crossing every which way.

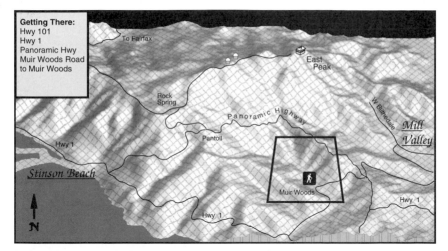

Getting There:
Hwy 101
Hwy 1
Panoramic Hwy
Muir Woods Road
to Muir Woods

To Fairfax

East
Peak

Rock
Spring

Panoramic Highway

W Blithedale

Mill
Valley

Pantoll

Hwy 1

Stinson Beach

Muir Woods

Hwy 1

Hwy 1

N

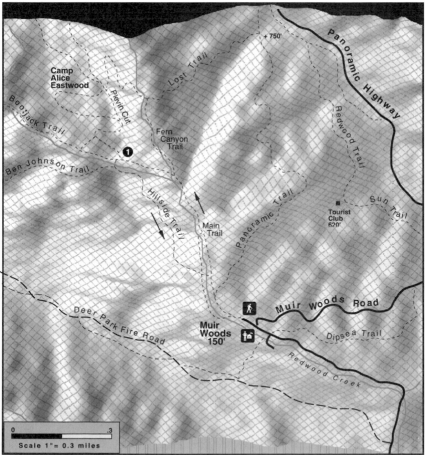

Panoramic Highway

+ 750'

Lost Trail

**Camp
Alice
Eastwood**

Plevin Cut

Redwood Trail

Boojack Trail

Fern
Canyon
Trail

Ben Johnson Trail

❶

Sun Trail

Hillside Trail

Panoramic Trail

Tourist
Club
620'

Main
Trail

Muir Woods Road

Deer Park Fire Road

**Muir
Woods
150'**

Dipsea Trail

Redwood Creek

0   .3
Scale 1" = 0.3 miles

12

4 Muir Woods - Fern Canyon Trails

Distance: 3.6 miles   Shaded: 100%
Elevation Change: 300'
Rating: Hiking - 9   Running - 9
When to Go: Excellent anytime, best in February and March.

This is a great redwood forest hike that leaves the crowded Muir Woods floor to explore Fern Canyon and Camp Alice Eastwood.

0.0 Start at the Muir Woods parking lot. Follow the signed Main trail along the right side of Redwood Creek.

0.7 Junction. Take the Fern Canyon trail right along the small creek. Watch for white trillium in March and the striking pink clintonia in April.

1.1 Junction #1 and bridge. Bear left down the 50' picturesque wood-plank bridge. Continue upstream on the left bank to another junction. Then, either take the shortcut up the stairs, or go slightly further upstream. Look for iris as the trail climbs through the redwoods.

1.8 Plevin Cut and Camp Alice Eastwood junctions #2. At the first junction, continue right to the parking area. The camp, named for Alice Eastwood, avid botanist, writer and hiker, was dedicated in 1949 on her 90th birthday.

This was also the location of the Muir Woods Inn, which served visitors who coasted down on gravity cars in the early 1900s.

From the camp, cross the paved parking circle to Camp Eastwood Rd signed to Muir Woods. The road starts downhill passing through broom, madrone, manzanita, oak and yerba santa.

Muir Woods Inn 1908

2.5 Junction #3. Take the signed Bootjack Spur trail right past a large lichen-covered redwood tree down to Redwood Creek, then go left and head downstream. Look for spawning salmon in late winter.

2.7 Junction and park boundary. Continue along the creek.

3.1 Bridge and Cathedral Grove. Cross the bridge to return down the right side of Redwood Creek. Look for redwood burls. Further ahead lies Bohemian Grove with some of the tallest trees in the park at 260'.

3.6 Snack shop, gift shop, restroom facilities and parking lot.

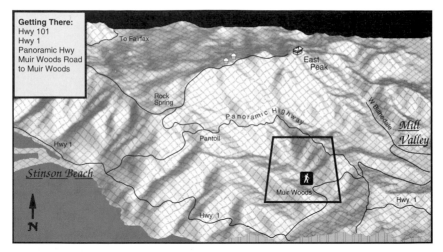

Getting There:
Hwy 101
Hwy 1
Panoramic Hwy
Muir Woods Road
to Muir Woods

To Fairfax

East
Peak

Rock
Spring

Panoramic Highway

W Blithedale

*Mill
Valley*

Pantoll

Hwy 1

Stinson Beach

Hwy 1

Muir Woods

Hwy 1

N

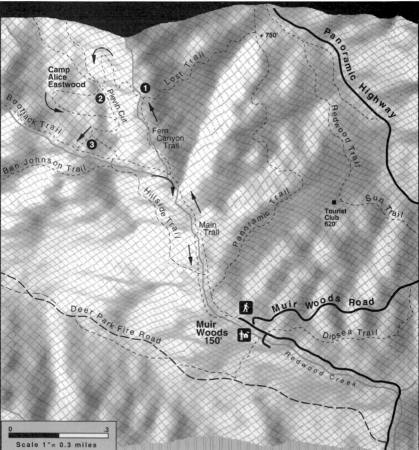

+ 750'

Panoramic Highway

Camp
Alice
Eastwood

Lost Trail

Plevin Cut

①

②

Bootjack Trail

③

Fern
Canyon
Trail

Redwood Trail

Sun Trail

Ben Johnson Trail

Hillside Trail

Panoramic Trail

Tourist
Club
620'

Main
Trail

Muir Woods Road

Deer Park Fire Road

Muir
Woods
150'

Dipsea Trail

Redwood Creek

0   .3
Scale 1"= 0.3 miles

14

5   Panoramic - Redwood - Sun Trails

Distance: 4.2 miles   Shaded: 70%
Elevation Change: 700'   One short steep section.
Rating: Hiking - 9   Running - 6   May be impassable, see note.
When to Go: Best February to April for flowers.

This is a great hike out of Muir Woods into mixed conifers, then on to
the Sun trail where wildflowers start in February.

Note: Sections of the Sun trail may be overgrown with French broom
and impassable. The hike is included here assuming that the trail will
be clear. It also serves as an example of the problems with broom.

0.0 At the Muir Woods entrance, take the Main trail up the right side
of Redwood Creek past magnificent redwoods.

0.2 Junction #1. Take the signed Panoramic trail right for a long
steady climb. In February, watch for pink trillium and blue hound's
tongue among the ferns, tanoak and redwoods.

1.5 Junction with Lost trail. Stay right and continue uphill. Look for
chaparral being overgrown by taller trees: bay, fir and redwood.

1.8 Junction and highway. Take the signed Panoramic trail right.
(The Panoramic trail formerly was called Ocean View trail.)

2.1 Junction #2. Bear right, downhill on the
signed Redwood trail.

2.4 Bench. Here is a good spot to enjoy the
views across Muir Woods to the ocean. Notice the
Douglas fir about to overgrow chaparral shrubs. In
spring, look for red Indian paintbrush.

2.8 Junction at the Tourist Club. This club was
founded in 1912 by German immigrants as a
branch of a European hiking club. The club is

Indian Paintbrush

private, but often sells refreshments on weekends. The trail continues
above the club to the road and then heads left for 100' to the Sun trail.

2.9 Junction #3. Head right on the Sun trail which earns its name by
skirting the south-facing hillside overlooking Muir Woods. Wildflowers
begin in February, building to a peak in April. (In a few years, the
flowers will be crowded out by invasive French broom.)

3.5 Junction. Follow the signed Dipsea trail right as it drops steeply
down the hillside and crosses the highway into a bay-filled ravine.

4.2 Parking lot, snack shop, gift shop and restroom facilities.

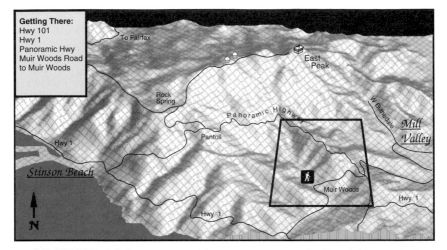

Getting There:
Hwy 101
Hwy 1
Panoramic Hwy
Muir Woods Road
to Muir Woods

To Fairfax

East Peak

Rock Spring

Panoramic Highway

W Blithedale

Mill Valley

Pantoll

Hwy 1

Stinson Beach

Muir Woods

Hwy 1

Hwy 1

N

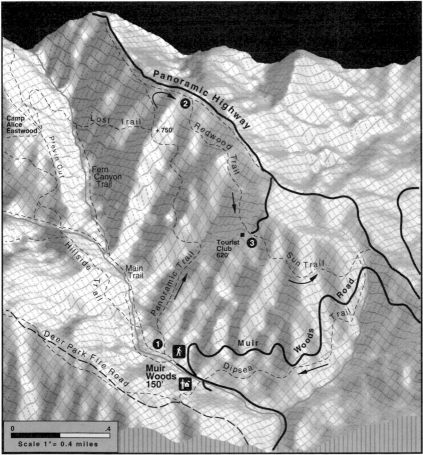

Panoramic Highway

Camp Alice Eastwood

Lost Trail

+ 750'

Redwood Trail

Pievin Cut

Fern Canyon Trail

Hillside Trail

Main Trail

Panoramic Trail

Tourist Club 620'

Sun Trail

Muir Woods Road

Deer Park Fire Road

Muir Woods 150'

Dipsea

0   .4
Scale 1" = 0.4 miles

16

6 Muir Woods - TCC - Dipsea Trails

Distance: 6.3 miles   Shaded: 70%
Elevation Change: 1200'   Steep in places.
Rating: Hiking - 10   Running - 7
When to Go: Good anytime, best in April after the bridge opens.

A dramatic hike into dense redwood forest with plunging creek, then down an open ridge with views and flowers, and into a lush canyon.

0.0 Start at the Muir Woods parking lot. Check at the kiosk to see if the Dipsea trail bridge is open. Follow the Main trail along the right side of Redwood Creek.

0.9 Junction #1. Take the signed Bootjack trail along the right side of Redwood Creek. Notice the light-green leaves of western azalea, hazel and big leaf maple against the dark-green, redwood needles.

1.3 Slides. Downed trees and large boulders testify to the power of fast-moving water. Look for white milkmaids, pink sorrel and trillium.

2.3 Van Wyck Meadow and junction #2. This meadow with its large picturesque rock and "population sign" has often served as a gathering and resting spot. Continue past the trail right and take the signed TCC trail left over the creek.

2.8 Manzanita. Notice the dead manzanita from an old chaparral community. Now, ferns and huckleberry lie under the conifers.

3.7 Junction #3 with the Stapelveldt trail. First go left, then right to take the signed TCC trail towards the Dipsea trail.

4.1 Junction #4. Eventually, we'll take the Dipsea trail left down to Muir Woods. However, now go right, uphill 200' to the hilltop for great views and wildflowers. This hill is known as "Cardiac Hill" to the 1500 Dipsea runners who struggle up from Muir Woods each June. Now backtrack down the trail and follow the Dipsea trail to the road. Watch for red columbine along the road in late spring.

4.5 Junction. Leave the road and go right down the Dipsea trail. The trail and the road (Deer Park FR) intersect several times.

4.7 Open hillside. This grassy ridge is called "Hogsback" by Dipsea runners. It is said to be where the Dipsea race is won or lost.

5.9 Junction #5. Take the trail left, down into a moist canyon filled with bay, hazel, berries and ferns. If the bridge is out, take the road.

6.2 Bridge. Cross the creek under red alders and head left.

6.3 Back at Muir Woods with full facilities.

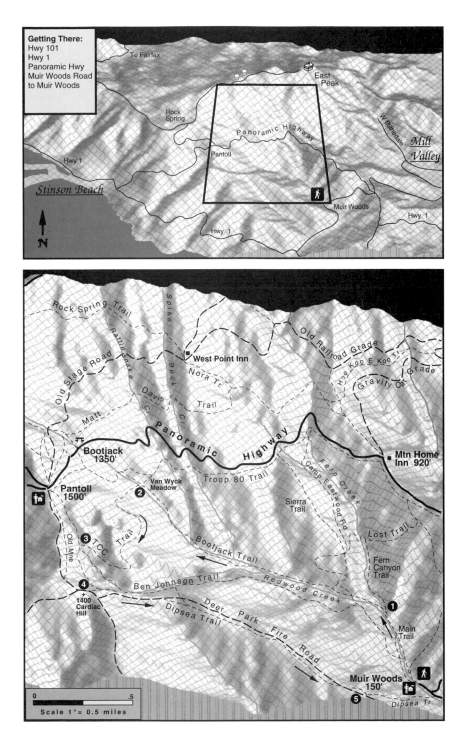

Getting There:
Hwy 101
Hwy 1
Panoramic Hwy
Muir Woods Road
to Muir Woods

To Fairfax

East Peak

Rock Spring

Panoramic Highway

Pantoll

W Blithedale

Mill Valley

Stinson Beach

Hwy 1

Muir Woods

Hwy 1

Hwy 1

N

Rock Spring Trail

Spike

Old Stage Road

Rattlesnake

Matt

Davis

Buck

Nora Tr

Trail

West Point Inn

Old Railroad Grade

Hog Koo E Koo Tr

Gravity Ca

Grade

Panoramic Highway

Bootjack 1350'

Troop 80 Trail

Mtn Home Inn 920'

Van Wyck Meadow

Pantoll 1500'

2

Fern Creek

Camp Eastwood Rd

Sierra Trail

Old Mne

3 TCC

Trail

Bootjack Trail

Lost Trail

Fern Canyon Trail

4

+ 1400 Cardiac Hill

Ben Johnson Trail

Redwood Creek

Deer Park Fire Road

Dipsea Trail

1

Main Trail

Muir Woods 150'

5

Dipsea Tr

0   .5

Scale 1"= 0.5 miles

18

7 Panoramic - Lost - Sierra Trails

Distance: 3.2 miles   Shaded: 60%
Elevation Change: 600'   One very steep section.
Rating: Hiking - 9   Running - 6
When to Go: Good anytime, best January to March.

This is a great hike that descends steeply into Fern Canyon, then gradually climbs back through chaparral and redwoods.

0.0 From the north end of the parking lot opposite the Mtn Home Inn, take the signed Trestle trail down the stairs. At the road, head left past chaparral consisting of manzanita and chamise.

0.1 Gate and junction. Take the signed Panoramic trail right past broom which may crowd the trail. Good views towards the ocean.

0.2 Junction #1. Take the Panoramic trail (originally called the Ocean View trail) right towards Muir Woods. Up ahead, Douglas fir has invaded and overgrown a chaparral area.

0.5 Junction. At the redwood grove, take the Lost trail right. This trail was constructed in 1914 by members of the Tourist Club. It is very steep in places and was blocked (hence "lost") for a long time by a massive slide in the1930s.

1.1 Junction and bridge. Bear right down the 50' bridge and continue upstream along the left bank of Fern Creek. The hike came down the south-facing hill through fir and bay. Now it climbs the north-facing hill through redwoods. Notice how many redwoods are burned on the uphill side where forest debris or duff collected.

1.7 Plevin Cut and Camp Eastwood junctions #2. At the first junction, go right up to Camp Eastwood, then go right again across the parking circle and take the signed Sierra trail up the dirt road.

1.8 Water tank. At the water tank and bench, the road abruptly ends and a trail swings in and out of the transition zone between two unlikely bedfellows, redwood and chaparral. Look for huckleberry bushes, which ripen in late summer.

Huckleberry

2.3 Chinquapin. The trail passes a small grove of chinquapin with 2 inch leaves, green on top and gold underneath.

2.4 Junction #3. Head right on Troop 80 trail towards Mtn Home.

2.8 Fern Creek and junction. Go left on the paved road.

3.2 Stairs. Take the stairs back up to the parking area.

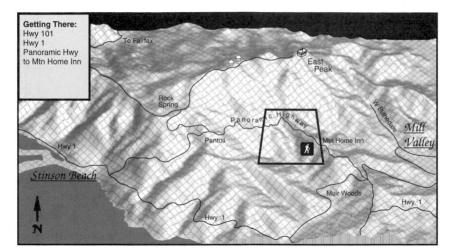

Getting There:
Hwy 101
Hwy 1
Panoramic Hwy
to Mtn Home Inn

To Fairfax

East
Peak

Rock
Spring

Panoramic Highway

Pantoll

Mtn Home Inn

W Blithedale

Mill
Valley

Hwy 1

Stinson Beach

Muir Woods

Hwy 1

Hwy 1

N

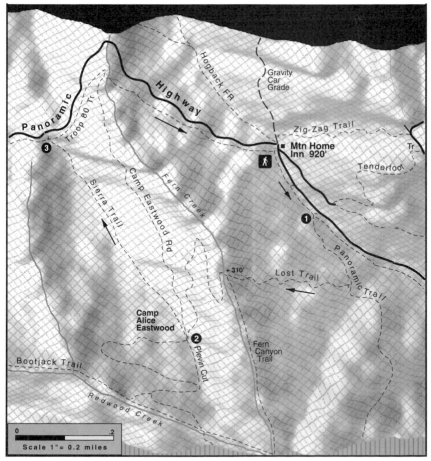

Panoramic

Highway

Hogback FR

Gravity
Car
Grade

Troop 80 Tr

Zig-Zag Trail

Tr

❸

■ Mtn Home
Inn 920'

Tenderfoot

Sierra Trail

Camp Eastwood Rd

Fern Creek

❶

Panoramic Trail

+310'

Lost Trail

Camp
Alice
Eastwood

❷

Plevin Cut

Fern
Canyon
Trail

Bootjack Trail

Redwood Creek

0   .2
Scale 1" = 0.2 miles

20

8 Mtn Home Inn to East Peak

Distance: 4.7 miles   Shaded: 30%
Elevation Change: 1700'   Very steep in places.
Rating: Hiking - 9   Running - 5
When to Go: Best on cool, clear, calm winter days.

This is the shortest and quickest hike to the top of Mt Tam. It offers great exercise and spectacular views in all directions.

0.0 Start at the Mtn Home Inn and head north across the highway and up the paved road towards the fire station. Take the Hogback FR past the fire station and up past three water tanks.

0.3 Junction with the Matt Davis trail. Continue up Hogback, which gets steeper as it passes by manzanita, oak, madrone, bay and fir.

0.6 Junction #1. Take the Old Railroad Grade left for a more gradual climb. The trail provides sweeping views in chaparral areas, then enters Fern Canyon with redwoods and occasional madrones.

1.0 Junction. Take the signed Fern Creek trail on the right and start a steep climb up the right side of the creek.

1.2 Creek crossing and junction #2. Tall chain ferns mark an uncertain creek crossing. About 100 yds beyond the crossing, the trail enters a dense stand of bay trees, then veers right to pass a blue water tank and the signed Tavern Pump trail.

The hike continues on Fern Creek trail up the left side of the creek along side a metal water pipe, then heads west out of the canyon.

1.7 Junction with Ridgecrest Road. Cross the road, take the stairs to the parking lot and head towards the picnic area and East Peak.

1.8 Junction. Take the signed Plankwalk trail up the north side.

2.0 East Peak and fire lookout station at 2571'. Stunning views!

2.2 East Peak parking lot. The small Visitor Center is usually open weekends from 12 - 4 pm. Take the one-way paved road to the west.

2.4 Two junctions #3. Take the Old Railroad Grade left.

3.1 Junction. Take the signed Miller trail left. The upper 200 yds of the trail is steep and dangerous with ruts and loose rocks. Once the trail enters an oak forest, the going is easier. Creek crossings ahead.

3.6 Junction. Take the Old Railroad Grade left to go downhill.

4.1 Junction #1. Take the Hogback trail right for a steep descent.

4.7 Mtn Home Inn parking area with restrooms and water.

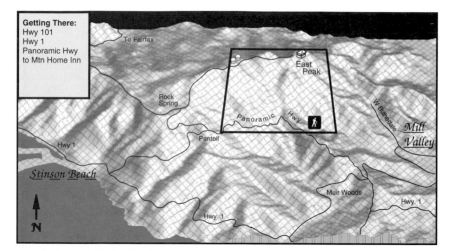

Getting There:
Hwy 101
Hwy 1
Panoramic Hwy
to Mtn Home Inn

To Fairfax

East
Peak

Rock
Spring

Panoramic Hwy

W Blithedale

Mill
Valley

Pantoll

Hwy 1

Stinson Beach

Muir Woods

Hwy 1

Hwy 1

N

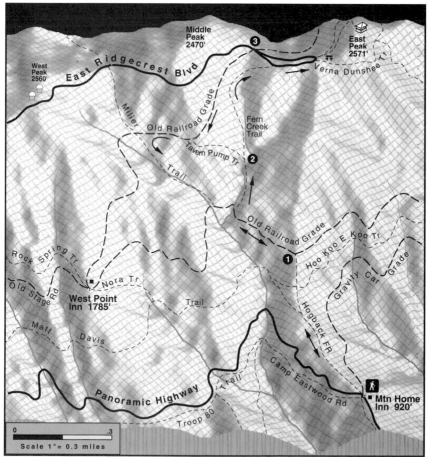

Middle
Peak
2470'

East
Peak
2571'

East Ridgecrest Blvd

Verna Dunshee

West
Peak
2560'

Miller

Old Railroad Grade

Fern
Creek
Trail

Tavern Pump Tr

Trail

Old Railroad Grade

Hoo Koo E Koo Tr

Gravity Car Grade

Rock Spring Tr

Nora Tr

West Point
Inn 1785'

Trail

Hogback FR

Old Stage Rd

Matt

Davis

Camp Eastwood Rd

Mtn Home
Inn 920'

Panoramic Highway

Troop 80

Trail

0   .3
Scale 1" = 0.3 miles

22

9 Matt Davis - Troop 80 Trails

Distance: 5.0 miles   Shaded: 60%
Elevation Change: 550'
Rating: Hiking - 9   Running - 8
When to Go: Good in winter and spring for views, sun and creeks.

This is a great hike along south-facing ridges, into redwood canyons and over cascading creeks, offering views to the city and coast.

0.0 From the north end of the parking lot opposite the Mtn Home Inn, cross the highway and take the paved road up past the fire station.

0.3 Water tank and junction #1. Just past the 3rd water tank, take the signed Matt Davis trail left towards the west. Good views south. Matt Davis, known as the "dean of trail workers", lived in a small cabin he built above Bootjack Camp. He was paid by the Tamalpais Conservation Club to work on trails; he built this trail in the 1920s.

0.6 Fern Creek. The concrete weir above the bridge was part of a water intake system that is no longer used.

Are the densely-packed, skinny redwoods young trees or stunted growth? Old-timers report similar groves 50 years ago.

1.3 Junction with the Nora trail. Cross the bridge and continue west.

1.9 Fire! Bare branches mark the remains of a 1984 controlled burn. The Water District considers these burns necessary to reduce the fire fuel load. After the burn, monkeyflower was the first major species to return. Now, chamise covers most of the hill.

2.6 Bootjack picnic area and junction #2. Follow the paved path through the picnic area down to the parking lot. Cross Panoramic Hwy and take the signed Bootjack trail downhill.

2.7 Junction with the Alpine trail. Continue downhill under redwoods.

3.0 Van Wyck Meadow and junction #3. The meadow, originally called Lower Rattlesnake Camp, was renamed for Sidney M. Van Wyck, president of the TCC in 1920-21. At the large rock in the center of the meadow, take a spur trail left, east towards the Troop 80 trail and Mtn Home Inn.

3.1 Junction and plaque. At the bottom of some steps, a plaque dedicates a Douglas fir tree to World War I veterans. Continue straight on the Troop 80 trail, built by the Ingleside Boy Scout Troop.

4.5 Junction with the paved Camp Eastwood road. Head left uphill.

5.0 Junction, stairs and the Mtn Home Inn parking area.

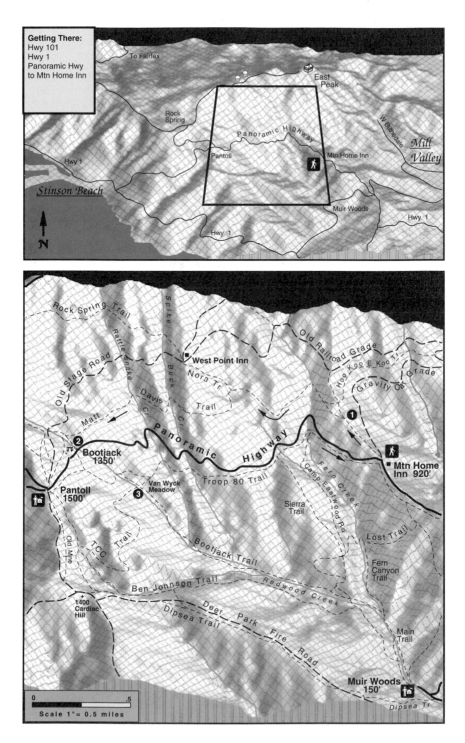

Getting There:
Hwy 101
Hwy 1
Panoramic Hwy
to Mtn Home Inn

To Fairfax

East
Peak

Rock
Spring

Panoramic Highway

Pantoll

Mtn Home Inn

W Blithedale

Mill
Valley

Hwy 1

Stinson Beach

Muir Woods

Hwy 1

Hwy 1

N

Rock Spring Trail

Spike

Old Stage Road

Rattle Snake

Davis

Buck

Matt

West Point Inn

Nora Tr

Trail

Old Railroad Grade

Hoo Koo E Koo Tr

Gravity Ca Grade

Panoramic Highway

Bootjack
1350'

Troop 80 Trail

Fern Creek

Mtn Home
Inn 920'

Pantoll
1500'

Van Wyck
Meadow

Camp Eastwood Rd

Sierra
Trail

Lost Trail

Old Mne

TCC

Trail

Bootjack Trail

Redwood Creek

Fern
Canyon
Trail

Ben Johnson Trail

1400
Cardiac
Hill

Dipsea Trail

Deer   Park   Fire   Road

Main
Trail

Muir Woods
150'

Dipsea Tr

0   .5

Scale 1" = 0.5 miles

24

10 Old RR Grade to West Point Inn

Distance: 3.8 miles   Shaded: 50%
Elevation Change: 800'
Rating: Hiking - 7   Running - 8   Heavy bicycle traffic weekends.
When to Go: Best on a clear day in fall, winter or spring.

This often-used route provides the shortest round trip to West Point Inn while offering great views east and south.

0.0 Start at the parking lot opposite the Mtn Home Inn. Cross the highway and take the paved road up towards the fire station. The road turns into Hogback FR, also called Throckmorton FR, which once led hikers all the way to East Peak, but is now closed for erosion control beyond Old Railroad Grade.

0.3 Two water tanks and junction. Continue up Hogback, which gets steeper here, providing an opportunity to enjoy some great views.

0.5 Junction #1. Turn left on the Old Railroad Grade which climbs gradually; the grade is never more than 7%. The entire 8.1 miles of road and track from downtown Mill Valley to East Peak took just six months to build in 1896.

0.9 Junction with Fern Creek trail. Just past the main ravine, look for a small spring supporting chain ferns.

2.0 Junction #2 and West Point Inn. This historic railroad tavern, built in 1904, was a restaurant and stopover point for passengers taking the stage to Bolinas and Willow Camp (later Stinson Beach).

West Point Inn

The inn was called West Point Inn because this is the westernmost point of the Old Railroad Grade.

For many years, the cast of the Mountain Play stayed at the inn the week before the play and walked to rehearsals each morning.

To continue the hike, take the signed Nora trail located in front of the inn. This well-maintained trail descends under a canopy of chaparral, then enters a grove of skinny redwoods.

2.5 Junction #3. Take the signed Matt Davis trail left.

3.5 Junction and water tanks. Take the Hogback FR downhill right.

3.8 Back at the parking lot with water and restrooms.

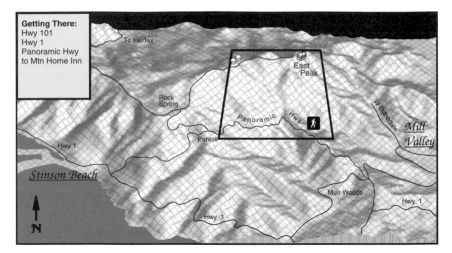

Getting There:
Hwy 101
Hwy 1
Panoramic Hwy
to Mtn Home Inn

To Fairfax

East
Peak

Rock
Spring

Panoramic   Hwy

Pantoll

W. Blithedale

*Mill
Valley*

Hwy 1

Stinson Beach

Muir Woods

Hwy 1

Hwy 1

N

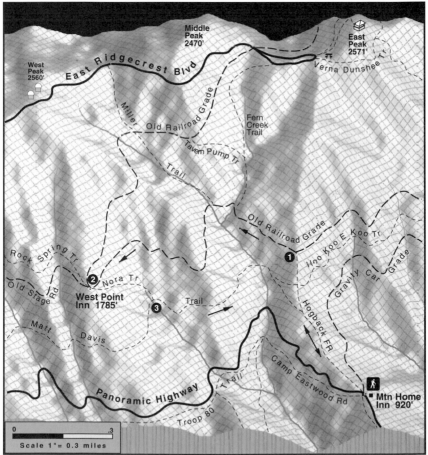

Middle
Peak
2470'

East
Peak
2571'

West
Peak
2560'

East Ridgecrest Blvd

Verna Dunshee Tr

Miller

Old Railroad Grade

Fern
Creek
Trail

Tavern Pump Tr

Trail

Old Railroad Grade

Hoo Koo E Koo Tr

Gravity Car

Grade

Rock Spring Tr

❶

❷ Nora Tr

West Point
Inn 1785'

❸   Trail

Hogback FR

Old Stage Rd

Matt   Davis

Panoramic Highway

Trail

Camp Eastwood Rd

Mtn Home
Inn 920'

Troop 80

0   .3
Scale 1"= 0.3 miles

26

11 TCC - Alpine Trails

Distance: 3.5 miles   Shaded: 90%
Elevation Change: 500'
Rating: Hiking - 9   Running - 9
When to Go: Good anytime, best in early spring.
This is a good hike exploring the dense woods east of Pantoll.
Cardiac Hill on the Dipsea Trail provides vistas and wildflowers.

0.0 Start at the Bootjack parking lot. Cross the highway and take the signed Bootjack trail towards Van Wyck Meadow. The trail drops steeply down past Douglas fir and bay into redwood forest. In early spring, look for white milkmaids and blue hound's tongue.

0.1 Junction with Alpine trail. Bear left to cross two small bridges ahead. Watch for white fairy bells and pink trillium.

0.4 Junction #1. Just past the bench and western azalea shrubs, continue right on the Bootjack trail. The trail goes along side moss-covered boulders, then down past a brown sandstone slab.

0.5 Junction and Van Wyck Meadow. Take the signed TCC trail right, across the creek and into redwoods. The TCC trail was built in 1918 and named for the Tamalpais Conservation Club, often called the "Guardians of the Mountain" for their conservation activities.

1.0 Manzanita. Notice the dead manzanitas from an old chaparral community. Now, ferns and huckleberry lie under the conifers.

1.9 Junction #2 with Stapelveldt trail. First go left, then right to take the signed TCC trail towards the Dipsea trail.

2.3 Junction. Take the Dipsea trail right uphill.

2.4 Junction #3 and hill. Congratulations! You have just climbed "Cardiac", as it's called by the throng of Dipsea runners who climb 1200' out of Muir Woods each June. Go right on the road.

2.5 Junction with Old Mine Rd. Bear right into Douglas fir and bay.

2.7 Junction. Take the Old Mine trail right. Up ahead, an 1863 mining claim was staked out in search of gold and silver.

3.0 Pantoll and junction #4. Water, tables and restrooms. Continue past the ranger station and take the signed Alpine trail just before the highway. The trail follows the road downhill.

3.4 Junction. Take the signed Bootjack trail left.

3.5 Back at Bootjack with water, tables and restrooms.

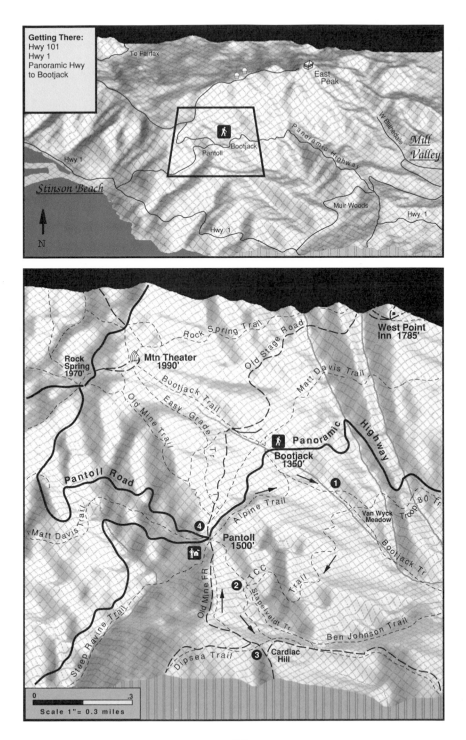

To Fairfax

East
Peak

W Blithedale

Mill Valley

Panoramic Highway

Pantoll   Bootjack

Hwy 1

Stinson Beach

N

Muir Woods

Hwy 1

Hwy 1

Rock Spring Trail

Old Stage Road

West Point
Inn 1785'

Rock
Spring
1970'

Mtn Theater
1990'

Matt Davis Trail

Bootjack Trail

Easy Grade Tr.

Old Mine Trail

Panoramic

Highway

Bootjack
1350'

1

Pantoll Road

Van Wyck
Meadow

Troop 80 Tr

Matt Davis Trail

4

Alpine Trail

Bootjack Tr

Pantoll
1500'

2

T.C.C.

Old Mine FR

Trail

Stapelveldt Tr

Steep Ravine Trail

Ben Johnson Trail

Dipsea Trail

3   Cardiac
Hill

0   .3

Scale 1" = 0.3 miles

28

12 Bootjack - Rock Spring Trails

Distance: 4.1 miles   Shaded: 60%
Elevation Change: 600'
Rating: Hiking - 8   Running - 7
When to Go: Good any cool, clear day, best February to April.

This is a good sunshine hike mostly through chaparral, first climbing to the Mtn Theater, then to West Point Inn and back.

0.0 Start at the Bootjack parking lot. Take the signed Bootjack trail towards Mtn Theater. Beyond the picnic area, two trails start uphill. Take the right trail and climb into oak-bay woodland.

0.2 Junction #1 with Old Stage Rd. In the early 1900s, a stage coach made a daily run from West Point Inn to Stinson Beach. Our hike just crosses the road. Go left on the road 20', then right 20', then left again to continue on the Bootjack trail. In early spring, look for blue hound's tongue, white milkmaids and purple iris.

0.7 Junction and Mtn Theater. Turn right at the junction and head towards the theater. Go up to the top of the theater to enjoy a unique setting and view. This natural amphitheater has been the site of spring plays since 1913. To continue the hike, go across the top to the northeast corner of the theater. See map inset, Hike 13.

0.8 Junction #2. Take the Rock Spring trail towards West Point Inn. This south-facing trail gradually descends through chaparral and wooded ravines. Watch for orange monkeyflower, tree poppy, blue-eyed grass, white Oakland star tulip and red Indian warrior.

1.4 Rocky knoll. Great views to San Francisco and the East Bay.

2.3 West Point Inn. Water, restrooms and beverages are available on most weekends. A pancake breakfast is served once a month from May to September in this glorious setting. To continue the hike, take the signed Nora trail in front of the picnic area.

2.8 Junction #3. Take the Matt Davis trail right over the bridge, out of the redwoods, and into a mixture of oak, huckleberry, manzanita and chamise with occasional Douglas fir and bay trees.

3.3 Controlled burn area. The last major fire on the mountain was in 1945. Now, controlled burns are necessary to reduce the fire danger.

3.7 Bridge. The trail enters a ravine, crosses a bridge on Rattlesnake Creek, then goes up a rocky slope.

4.1 Back at Bootjack picnic area with restrooms, tables and water.

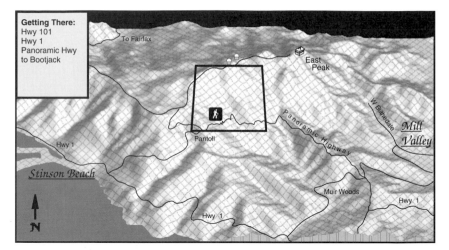

Getting There:
Hwy 101
Hwy 1
Panoramic Hwy
to Bootjack

To Fairfax

East
Peak

W Blithedale

*Mill
Valley*

Panoramic Highway

Pantoll

Stinson Beach

Muir Woods

Hwy 1

Hwy 1

Hwy 1

N

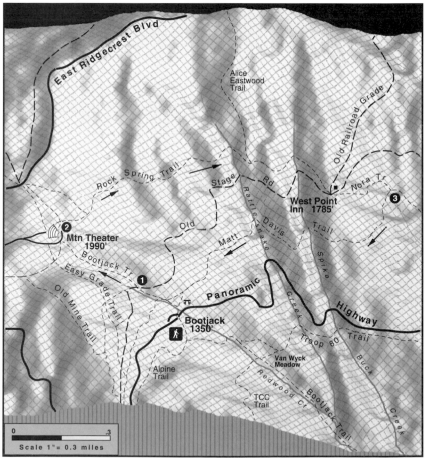

East Ridgecrest Blvd

Alice
Eastwood
Trail

Old Railroad Grade

Nora Tr.

Rock Spring Trail

Stage

Rd

West Point
Inn 1785'

❸

Mtn Theater
1990'

❷

Old

Davis

Rattlesnake

Matt

Trail

Spike

Bootjack Tr.

Easy Grade Trail

❶

Old Mine Trail

Panoramic

Creek

Highway

Bootjack
1350'

Troop 80

Trail

Buck

Van Wyck
Meadow

Alpine
Trail

Redwood Cr.

Bootjack Trail

Creek

TCC
Trail

0   .3

Scale 1" = 0.3 miles

30

13 Easy Grade to Mountain Theater

Distance: 2.2 miles   Shaded: 60%
Elevation Change: 500'
Rating: Hiking - 10   Running - 8
When to Go: Good any clear day, best in spring.

This short hike climbs from Pantoll through forest to the MtnTheater, then over open hills with magnificent views south and east.

0.0 Start at the Pantoll parking lot. Cross the highway, bear right and go along the paved section of the Old Stage Rd signed to East Peak. Immediately ahead, continue on the road past two junctions.

0.1 Junction. Take the signed Easy Grade trail left towards the Mtn Theater. The trail climbs up wooded hills with occasional views east.

0.3 Junction with Easy Grade Spur trail. Keep left at the Spur trail and straight up ahead. Watch for white milkmaids and iris.

0.8 Mtn Theater and junction. This natural amphitheater has been the site of plays since 1913. The present theater was built in 1934 using over 40,000 stones, some weighing 4000 lbs. Each stone is buried so that only a small fraction is visible. Water and restrooms nearby. To continue the hike, head up the right side of the theater, then back across the top and admire the views. Continue west on the paved road.

Map of Mtn Theater Area

1.0 Junction #1. Head left on the signed road to Madrone Grove and explore the hilltop covered with large madrone, oak and Douglas fir trees. To continue the hike, backtrack to the road and go left (west) through the gate, cross the highway and pick up the signed trail towards Rock Spring.

1.2 Rock Spring and junction #2. From the parking area, cross the highway, bear left and take the signed Mtn Theater fire trail uphill.

1.3 Junction with Old Mine trail. Bear right along the open hillside.

1.5 Rocky knoll and spectacular views!

1.9 Junction #3. Continue straight towards Pantoll and right ahead.

2.2 Back at Pantoll ranger station. Full facilities.

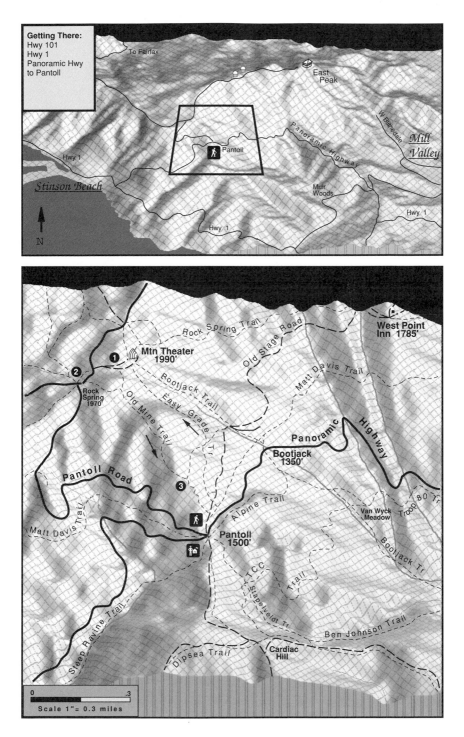

Getting There:
Hwy 101
Hwy 1
Panoramic Hwy
to Pantoll

To Fairfax

East Peak

Panoramic Highway

W Blithedale

Mill Valley

Pantoll

Hwy 1

Stinson Beach

Muir Woods

Hwy 1

Hwy 1

N

Rock Spring Trail

Old Stage Road

West Point Inn 1785'

Mtn Theater 1990'

❶

❷

Rock Spring 1970'

Bootjack Trail

Matt Davis Trail

Easy Grade

Old Mine Trail

Panoramic

Highway

Bootjack 1350'

❸

Pantoll Road

Van Wyck Meadow

Troop 80 Tr

Alpine Trail

Bootjack Tr

Matt Davis Trail

Pantoll 1500'

T.C.C. Trail

Stapelveldt Tr

Steep Ravine Trail

Ben Johnson Trail

Dipsea Trail

Cardiac Hill

0   .3
Scale 1"= 0.3 miles

32

14 Dipsea - Steep Ravine Trails

Distance: 3.6 miles   Shaded: 70%
Elevation Change: 1100'   Steep in places.
Rating: Hiking - 10   Running - 5
When to Go: Good in winter and spring, best on a clear April day.

This is a breathtaking hike through forest, along coastal hills, then up spectacular Steep Ravine. Good wildflowers and good views.

0.0 Start at the Pantoll parking lot. Take the paved road next to the ranger station south 200' to the signed Old Mine trail. Go left into Douglas fir forest with some oak and bay. In March, look for white zigadene, yellow buttercup, blue hound's tongue and purple iris.

0.2 Mining claim. In 1863, prospectors dug for gold and silver.

0.3 Junction. Continue south on the Old Mine Rd.

0.5 Junction with Dipsea Fire Rd. Stay left on the road.

0.6 Junction #1. Follow the Dipsea trail right. This trail is thought to be one of the oldest on the mountain. In 1905, it became part of the famous Dipsea race that covers 7.1 miles from downtown Mill Valley to Stinson Beach.

1.3 Junction #2. Take the Dipsea trail right towards Stinson Beach.

1.4 Fence. Bear right. The trail drops down through luxuriant growth kept moist by winter rain and summer fog. Ahead, the trail drops so steeply that it's hard to believe that 1500 Dipsea runners plunge through here at full speed each June.

Dipsea Race - June 1993

2.0 Junction #3 and bridge. Cross the bridge, go right on the Steep Ravine trail and enjoy the finest scenery on Mt Tam. Steep Ravine offers spectacular redwoods, ferns, mosses, berries, tumbled trees, wooden bridges, quiet pools and cascading waterfalls.

2.4 Notched redwood. A large redwood lying across the trail is notched to allow passage. As you duck, look for white fairy bells.

2.8 Ladder. Webb Creek is squeezed by large boulders. The only way up is to climb a 10' ladder.

3.6 Back at Pantoll with camping, restrooms, tables and water.

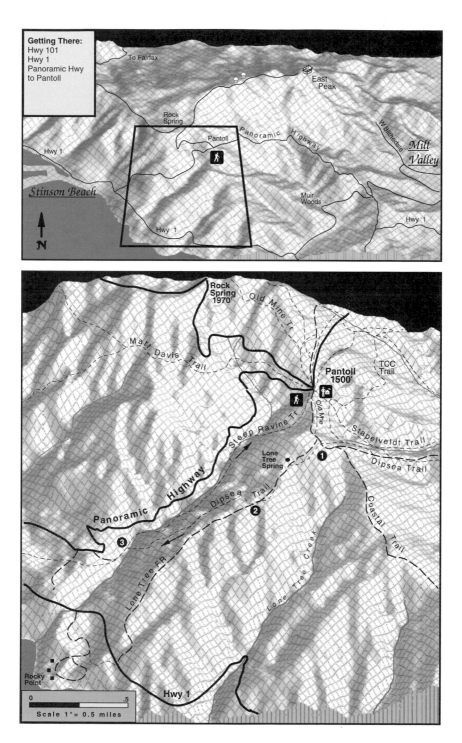

Getting There:
Hwy 101
Hwy 1
Panoramic Hwy
to Pantoll

To Fairfax

East Peak

Rock Spring

Pantoll

Panoramic Highway

W Blithedale

Mill Valley

Stinson Beach

N

Muir Woods

Hwy 1

Hwy 1

Rock Spring 1970'

Old Mine Tr.

Matt Davis Trail

Pantoll 1500'

TCC Trail

Steep Ravine Tr.

Old Me

Stapelveldt Trail

Lone Tree Spring

Dipsea Trail

❶

Panoramic Highway

Dipsea Trail

❷

Coastal Trail

❸

Lone Tree FR.

Lone Tree Creek

Rocky Point

Hwy 1

0   .5
Scale 1" = 0.5 miles

34

15 Matt Davis - Coastal - Cataract Trails

Distance: 6.6 miles   Shaded: 50%
Elevation Change: 700'
Rating: Hiking - 10   Running - 7   May be overgrown in summer.
When to Go: Best on a clear day in March or April.

Here is a magnificent hike through dense forest, past flowering hillsides, then along a refreshing creek. Spectacular views.

0.0 From the Pantoll parking lot, cross Panoramic Hwy and take the paved Pantoll Rd 200' uphill to the Matt Davis trail signed towards Stinson Beach. The trail starts out along open hillside, but soon enters dense woods of Douglas fir, oak and bay. Wildflowers along the trail include white zigadene, yellow poppy, yellow Mariposa lily, blue hound's tongue, blue-eyed grass, blue dicks and iris.

1.2 Open hillside. Leaving the woods, look for white popcorn flower, yellow buttercup, pink checkerbloom and lupine. Great views. Up ahead, a short spur trail leads left to a lookout point.

1.6 Junction #1. Stay right to climb gently on the Coastal trail. In summer, this trail is crowded with grasses, thistles and stickers.

2.4 Rock outcroppings. Green-grey lichens enjoy the cool and moist coastal climate on these small rocky patches.

3.3 Junction #2. Turn right and take the Willow Camp FR steeply up to the first knoll, then take the short trail left to Ridgecrest Blvd.

3.5 Highway junction. Continue on the dirt road to Laurel Dell.

3.8 Junction #3. A trail leads right, over the bridge on Cataract Creek. Go left on Cataract trail through the meadow to Laurel Dell.

4.1 Laurel Dell picnic area. Continue north on the Cataract trail.

4.2 Waterfalls and turnaround point. Beneath a big-leaf maple, moss-covered rocks and ferns, Cataract Creek starts its vigorous plunge to Alpine Lake. To continue the hike, backtrack south along the left side of Cataract Creek towards jct. #3 and Rock Spring.

4.6 Junction and airplane engine. About 100' past the bridge on the right, look for a Navy Corsair airplane engine down in the middle of the creek, the result of a mid-air plane collision October 4, 1945.

5.6 Rock Spring. Cross the highway, bear left and take the signed Mtn Theater fire trail uphill, then right on the Old Mine trail.

5.9 Rocky knoll and spectacular views. Continue downhill.

6.6 Back at Pantoll Ranger Station. Full facilities.

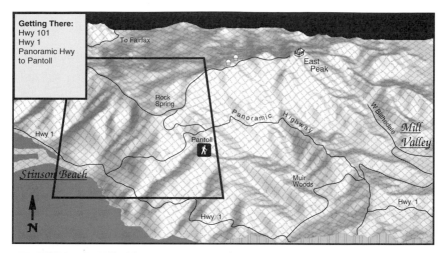

Getting There:
Hwy 101
Hwy 1
Panoramic Hwy
to Pantoll

To Fairfax

East
Peak

Rock
Spring

Panoramic Highway

Pantoll

W Blithedale

Mill Valley

Hwy 1

Stinson Beach

Muir
Woods

Hwy 1

Hwy 1

N

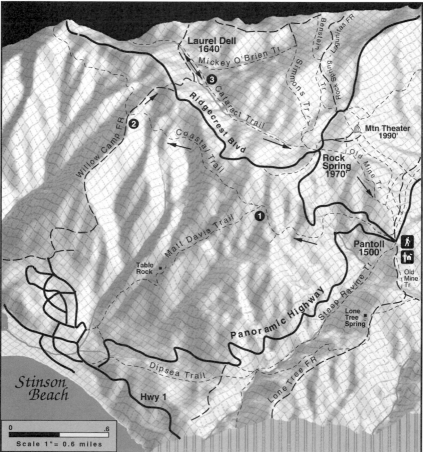

Benstein Tr.

Lounitas FR

Rock Spring Tr.

Laurel Dell
1640'

Mickey O'Brien Tr.

3

Cataract Trail

Simmons Tr.

Ridgecrest Blvd

Mtn Theater
1990'

Willow Camp FR

2

Coastal Trail

Old Mine Tr.

Rock
Spring
1970'

1

Matt Davis Trail

Pantoll
1500'

Table
Rock

Old
Mine
Tr.

Panoramic Highway

Steep Ravine Tr.

Lone
Tree
Spring

Stinson
Beach

Dipsea Trail

Lone Tree FR

Hwy 1

0 ——————— .6

Scale 1" = 0.6 miles

36

16 Matt Davis Trail to Stinson Beach

Distance: 7.0 miles   Shaded: 60%
Elevation Change: 1600'   Steep in places. Many stairs.
Rating: Hiking - 10   Running - 7
When to Go: Good anytime, best in winter and spring.

This strenuous, but spectacular hike, starts out on coastal hills, then descends to Stinson Beach and returns along scenic Steep Ravine.

0.0 From the Pantoll parking lot, cross Panoramic Hwy and take the paved Pantoll Rd 200' uphill to the signed Matt Davis trail heading west towards Stinson Beach.

0.4 Webb Creek. Mosses, chain ferns, bays and Douglas fir provide a woodsy setting next to bedrock carved by Webb Creek.

1.2 Open hillsides. Great views to Stinson Beach and Bolinas Mesa. Look for checkerbloom and lupine among the spring wildflowers.

1.6 Junction #1. Take the signed Matt Davis trail left towards Stinson Beach. The trail makes a gradual descent until it enters a Douglas fir forest where it drops more quickly. Lots of stairs.

3.5 Table Rock. At a fencepost under buckeye trees, take a spur trail 10' to the right to Table Rock. Great views of Bolinas Lagoon.

3.7 Bridge and junction #2. Go left across the creek and bridge. Up ahead, bear to the right at the Y-junction.

4.0 Paved street. The trail emerges on Belvedere Street. Continue west towards Shoreline Hwy. At the road, go left 100 yds, then take the first right to head past the Parkside Cafe to the beach entrance.

4.3 Stinson Beach State Park. The park has full facilities: grass, trees and shade, beach, swimming, water, food and restrooms. It offers a great place for resting and picnicking, although it may be crowded on summer weekends. After enjoying the beach, retrace your steps to Shoreline Hwy.

4.6 Shoreline Hwy. Head south for 300 yds along the highway to take the famed Dipsea trail towards Steep Ravine and Pantoll.

5.0 Open hillsides. Take the most prominent trail across the "moors" up towards the steps and fire road. Continue across the fire road.

5.6 Bridge and junction #3. Take the signed Steep Ravine trail left. This is a magnificent area offering an inspiring setting of redwoods, ferns, mosses, creeks and waterfalls.

7.0 Back at the Pantoll parking area with water and restrooms.

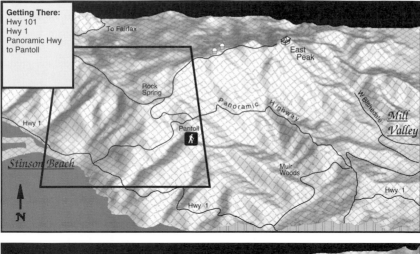

Getting There:
Hwy 101
Hwy 1
Panoramic Hwy
to Pantoll

To Fairfax

East Peak

Rock Spring

Panoramic Highway

W Blithedale

Mill Valley

Hwy 1

Pantoll

Stinson Beach

Muir Woods

Hwy 1

Hwy 1

N

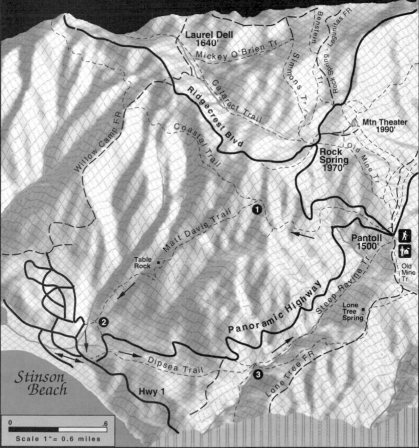

Laurel Dell
1640'

Mickey O'Brien Tr.

Benstein Tr.

Rock Spring FR

Laguntias FR

Cataract Trail

Simmons Tr.

Willow Camp FR

Ridgecrest Blvd

Coastal Trail

Mtn Theater
1990'

Old Mine Tr.

Rock
Spring
1970'

Malt Davis Trail

①

Table Rock

Pantoll
1500'

Old Mine Tr.

②

Sleep Ravine Tr.

Lone Tree Spring

Panoramic Highway

Lone Tree FR

Dipsea Trail

③

Stinson Beach

Hwy 1

0   .6
Scale 1" = 0.6 miles

38

17 Simmons - Music Camp - Cataract

Distance: 3.8 miles   Shaded: 60%
Elevation Change: 800'   Steep and rocky in places.
Rating: Hiking - 10   Running - 4
When to Go: Best in winter and spring after rain.

This is a great hike through woods and chaparral and along three cascading creeks to Barth's Retreat and Music Camp.

0.0 Start at the Rock Spring parking area and take the signed Cataract trail into the meadow. Up ahead, continue straight on the signed Simmons trail towards the Benstein trail.

0.2 Junction. Bear left on the signed Simmons trail and head downhill towards Ziesche Creek. Look for the coral root orchid in May.

0.3 Bridge and junction #1. Cross the bridge to make a steep climb up to a hilltop covered with tanoak and large Douglas fir trees.

0.4 Chaparral. The trail abruptly leaves the forest and enters a rocky serpentine slope, covered with chamise and Sargent cypress.

1.2 Barth's Retreat and junction #2. The trail drops down through Douglas fir, bay, oak and madrone to cross a creek at Barth's Retreat. Emil Barth, pianist and avid hiker, built his camp in the 1920s. To continue, take the dirt road north into coastal scrub.

1.3 Junction. Continue straight across the Laurel Dell FR and follow an uncertain path through chaparral and down into a rocky creek bed. Ahead, the trail descends along the left side of the creek.

1.5 Two creek crossings and junction #3. The trail crosses to the right of the creek, goes 30 yds, then returns to the left side of the creek and goes for 40 yds to a junction next to a double-trunked fir tree. Head left, away from the creek, for 50 yds to Music Camp.

1.6 Music Camp. This idyllic, hidden retreat, one of Mt Tam's many treasures, was built by music lover, Ben Schmidt, in the1950s. When ready to return, retrace your steps back up to Barth's Retreat.

1.8 Barth's Retreat. Take the Mickey O'Brien trail, which stays on the left side of Barth's Creek, downhill towards Laurel Dell.

2.6 Junction #4 with Cataract trail. Head left towards Rock Spring. About 100' past the bridge on the right, look for a Navy Corsair airplane engine down in the middle of the creek, the result of a mid-air plane collision October 4, 1945.

3.8 Parking area. Ocean view, tables and restrooms.

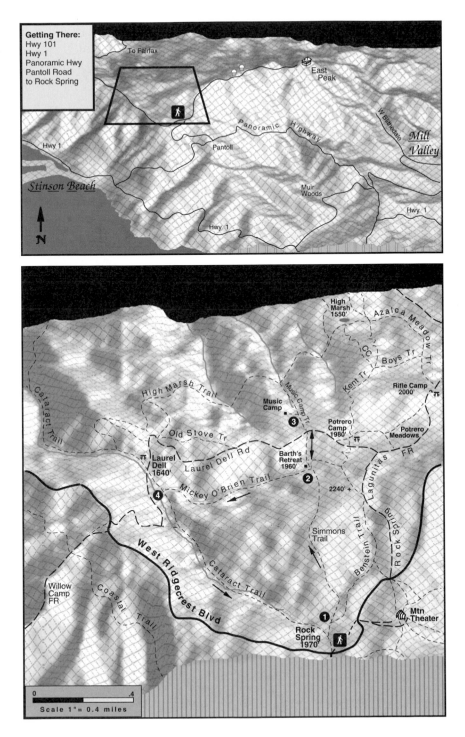

Getting There:
Hwy 101
Hwy 1
Panoramic Hwy
Pantoll Road
to Rock Spring

To Fairfax

East
Peak

Panoramic Highway

Pantoll

W Blithedale

Mill
Valley

Hwy 1

Stinson Beach

Muir
Woods

Hwy 1

Hwy 1

N

High
Marsh
1550'

Azalea Meadow Tr

CC

Boys Tr

Kent Tr

Rifle Camp
2000'

High Marsh Trail

Music Camp Tr

Music
Camp

❸

Cataract Trail

Old Stove Tr

Potrero
Camp
1980'

Potrero
Meadows

Laurel Dell Rd

Barth's
Retreat
1960'

❷

Laurel
Dell
1640'

Lagunitas FR

Mickey O'Brien Trail

2240' +

❹

Rock Spring

Simmons
Trail

Benstein Trail

West Ridgecrest Blvd

Cataract Trail

Willow
Camp
FR

Coastal Trail

Rock
Spring
1970'

❶

Mtn
Theater

0   .4

Scale 1" = 0.4 miles

40

18 Benstein - International Trails

Distance: 5.2 miles   Shady: 40%
Elevation Change: 600'   Steep in places.
Rating: Hiking - 8   Running - 7   Some bicycle traffic.
When to Go: Best when clear for views and late March for orchids.

This is a pleasant hike that explores woods and chaparral on both sides of the mountain offering great views and good wildflowers.

0.0 Start at the Rock Spring parking area and take the signed Cataract trail into the meadow. Up ahead, continue straight on the signed Simmons trail towards the Benstein trail.

0.2 Junction. Take the signed Benstein trail right into Douglas fir and tanoak trees and up past moss-covered rocks. In late March, look for the delicate and beautiful calypso orchid usually found under Douglas fir. It has a bright pink flower with a lower scoop-like petal colored to attract insects for pollination. The plant, also called "fairy slipper", is common in the Pacific northwest, but rare here.

Calypso Orchid

0.4 Junction with trail to the Mtn Theater. Continue left towards signed Potrero Meadows.

0.7 Junction #1. Go left on the Rock Spring - Lagunitas Rd.

1.3 Junction #2 and Rifle Camp. Go down through the picnic area, cross the creek and take the signed Northside trail into woods.

1.8 Views. Great views north, east and west. Continue straight across the serpentine ridgeline; notice the stunted Sargent cypress.

1.9 Junction #3. Take the signed International trail right. Notice the manzanita being succeeded by Douglas fir, oak and some nutmeg.

2.4 Junction with Ridgecrest Blvd. Cross the road and take the Miller trail down the rocky hillside. John Miller, who worked on trails for over 30 years, was injured while working here in 1947 at the age of 80.

2.7 Junction #4. Turn right and take the Old RR Grade downhill.

3.4 Junction and West Point Inn. Water, restroom, tables and view. To continue the hike, take the Rock Spring trail west of the inn.

4.9 Mtn Theater. Water, restrooms and picnic area. Continue right, around the top of the theater, and along the paved path to Ridgecrest Blvd. Cross the road and take the trail to Rock Spring.

5.2 Rock Spring parking area. Ocean view, tables and restrooms.

41

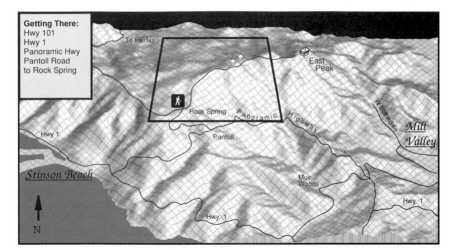

Getting There:
Hwy 101
Hwy 1
Panoramic Hwy
Pantoll Road
to Rock Spring

To Fairfax

East Peak

Rock Spring

Panoramic Highway

W Blithedale

Pantoll

Mill Valley

Stinson Beach

Muir Woods

Hwy 1

Hwy 1

Hwy 1

N

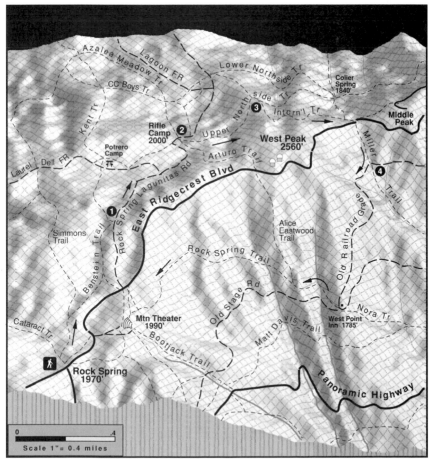

Azalea Meadow Tr

Lagoon FR

Lower Northside Tr

Colier Spring 1840'

CC Boys Tr

Northside Tr

Middle Peak

Kent Tr

Rifle Camp 2000' ②

Intern'l Tr ③

Upper

West Peak 2560'

Potrero Camp

Arturo Trail

Laurel Dell FR

Rock Spring Lagunitas Rd

East Ridgecrest Blvd

④

Miller Trail

Simmons Trail

①

Old Railroad Grade

Benstein Trail

Alice Eastwood Trail

Rock Spring Trail

Cataract Tr

Old Stage Rd

Nora Tr

Mtn Theater 1990'

West Point Inn 1785'

Bootjack Trail

Matt Davis Trail

Rock Spring 1970'

Panoramic Highway

0 .4
Scale 1" = 0.4 miles

42

19 Cataract - High Marsh - Kent Trails

Distance: 6.0 miles   Shaded: 90%
Elevation Change: 800'   Steep and rocky in places.
Rating: Hiking - 10   Running - 6
When to Go: Good anytime, great in winter and spring.

This is a magnificent hike that features creeks, forests, views and flowers in some of the most remote areas on the mountain.

0.0 Start at the Rock Spring parking area and take the Cataract trail down the left side of the meadow towards Cataract Creek. The Cataract trail offers some of the finest hiking on Mt Tam with pools, waterfalls, small meadows, wildflowers and Douglas fir forest.

1.2 Junction with Mickey O'Brien trail. This area can be soggy when wet. Continue straight. Good flowers in the meadow in spring.

1.3 Laurel Dell picnic area with tables and restrooms. From the picnic area, take the signed Cataract trail downstream.

1.5 Junction #1, bench and waterfalls. Here, Cataract Creek starts its dramatic plunge towards Alpine Lake. At the bench, take the High Marsh trail right and right again 100' ahead. The trail climbs past a down oak tree, then skirts an open hillside with great views north.

2.3 Junction with spur trail to Laurel Dell FR. Continue on the High Marsh trail which follows a roller-coaster pattern, downhill into forested ravines, then uphill to ridges covered with chaparral.

3.0 Creek and junction. A large 20' by 30' boulder in the streambed marks the trail right to Music Camp. Continue straight.

3.3 Unmarked junction. The Willow trail heads downhill left. Continue straight and slightly uphill past a small grove of madrone trees.

3.5 High Marsh and junction. The Cross Country Boys trail heads right and uphill. Continue straight as the trail skirts the marsh.

3.6 Junction #2. Take the signed Kent trail right which climbs slowly at first, then zig-zags up the ridge.

4.2 Junction. The CC Boys trail crosses here. Continue straight.

4.6 Potrero Camp and junction #3. Take the dirt road south to Laurel Dell FR, then go left 100' and take the signed Benstein trail uphill. The trail climbs into a serpentine outcropping with Sargent cypress trees.

5.3 Junction #4. Take the Rock Spring-Lagunitas FR right 100 yds, then head downhill on the signed Benstein trail.

6.0 Back at the Rock Spring parking area with restrooms.

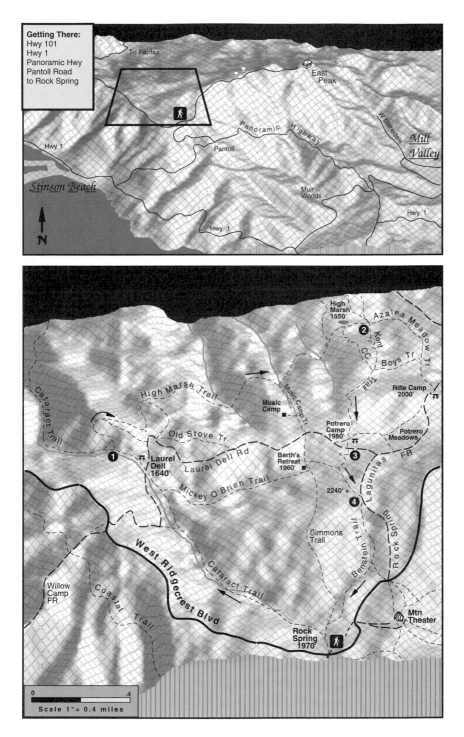

Getting There:
Hwy 101
Hwy 1
Panoramic Hwy
Pantoll Road
to Rock Spring

To Fairfax

East
Peak

W Blithedale

Panoramic Highway

Pantoll

Mill
Valley

Hwy 1

Stinson Beach

Muir
Woods

Hwy 1

Hwy 1

N

High
Marsh
1550'

Azalea Meadow Tr

Kent

CC

Boys Tr

Trail

High Marsh Trail

Cataract Trail

Rifle Camp
2000'

Music Camp Tr

Music
Camp

Old Stove Tr

Potrero
Camp
1980'

Potrero
Meadows

Laurel Dell Rd

Laurel Dell 1640'

Barth's
Retreat
1960'

Lagunitas FR

Mickey O'Brien Trail

2240' +

Rock Spring

Simmons
Trail

Benstein Trail

Willow
Camp
FR

West Ridgecrest Blvd

Cataract Trail

Coastal Trail

Mtn
Theater

Rock
Spring
1970'

0   .4
Scale 1"= 0.4 miles

44

20 East Peak Loop Trail

Distance: 0.7 miles   Shaded: 10%
Elevation Change: 50'
Rating: Hiking - 10   Running - 10   Paved.
When to Go: Great anytime on a clear, windless day.

This short hike on a paved path offers incomparable views of the San Francisco Bay Area. The flora is primarily chaparral.

0.0 From the East Peak parking lot, go east towards the restroom and take the signed Verna Dunshee trail to circle the peak counterclockwise. The concrete picnic area is all that remains of the Tamalpais Tavern, a restaurant and inn built by the railroad in the

1890s. It suffered serious damage in a forest fire in 1913 and again in a kitchen fire in 1923. Each time, it was quickly rebuilt and, because of its remote location, thrived during prohibition. In 1942, the tavern was leased to the army for barracks. After the war, it fell into disrepair and was destroyed.

Tamalpais Tavern 1922

0.1 View. Look down at Mesa Junction. Here you can see the Old Railroad Grade make its famous Double Bowknot, laying claim to the "Crookedest Railroad in the World."

0.2 Sunrise Point. On a clear day, this point offers one of the finest views in the world! Watch for turkey vultures soaring below you.

0.3 Junction and bench. Sometimes you can see mountain climbers practicing their skills on the jagged rocks above you.

Up ahead, the path rounds a bend opening up great vistas north. Vegetation is more robust here than on the south side.

0.5 Lakes. Good views of Bon Tempe and Lagunitas lakes and the hills of north Marin. On a crystal-clear day, you can see the geysers of Sonoma county puffing away.

0.6 Rocks. The red-brown rock outcroppings most common along the path are quartz-tourmaline. Inspect the various colored lichens making these rocks their home.

0.7 Parking area with tables, water and restrooms. A small visitor center and snackbar is usually open on weekends from 12-4 pm.

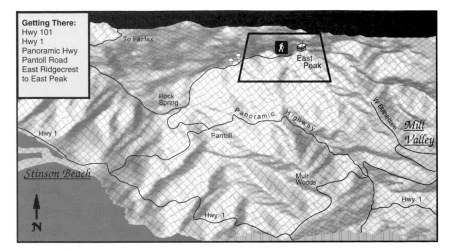

Getting There:
Hwy 101
Hwy 1
Panoramic Hwy
Pantoll Road
East Ridgecrest
to East Peak

To Fairfax

East Peak

Rock Spring

Panoramic Highway

Pantoll

W. Blithedale

Mill Valley

Hwy 1

Stinson Beach

Muir Woods

Hwy 1

Hwy 1

N

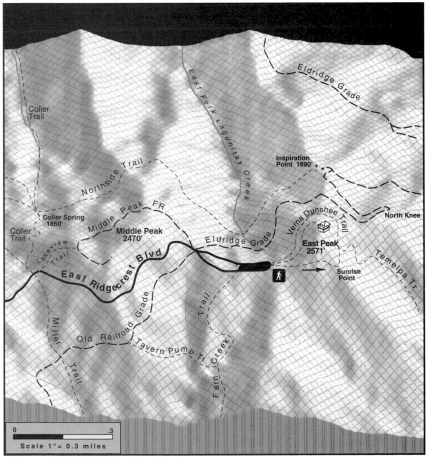

Colier Trail

Eldridge Grade

East Fork Lagunitas Creek

Northside Trail

Inspiration Point 1890'

Colier Spring 1860'

Middle Peak FR

Verna Dunshee Trail

North Knee

Colier Trail

Lakeview Trail

Middle Peak 2470'

Eldridge Grade

East Peak 2571'

East Ridgecrest Blvd

Temelpa Tr.

Sunrise Point

Miller Trail

Old Railroad Grade

Tavern Pump Tr.

Fern Creek Trail

Scale 1" = 0.3 miles
0   .3

46

21 Northside - Colier - Lakeview Trails

Distance: 4.3 miles   Shady: 70%
Elevation Change: 500'
Rating: Hiking - 8   Running - 4   Very rocky in places.
When to Go: Good anytime, best March to May after rain.
Wear sturdy boots to hike the rocky north slopes below East Peak.
Good chaparral, some redwoods and lots of oak and nutmeg.

0.0 From the East Peak parking lot, take the one-way paved road west, away from the restrooms.

0.3 Junction #1 with Eldridge Grade. Go through the gate and downhill past oak, chamise, manzanita, ceanothus, yerba santa and occasional chaparral pea. Spring wildflowers along the road include white milkmaids, modesty, yellow monkeyflower, red Indian warrior, Indian paintbrush and iris.

Watch for California nutmeg, a California endemic with flat, one-inch, sharp, green needles, common on this hike.

1.0 Hairpin turn. Continue around the hairpin turn. Up ahead, more moisture and better soil produce more luxuriant growth.

1.3 Junction #2. Take the Northside trail left toward Colier Spring.

1.4 Inspiration Point and great views. The hike leaves the road here and follows the narrow Northside trail, which starts out level and heads southwest into a canyon below East Peak.

3.1 Colier Spring and junction #3. Pause at the bench just below the spring to enjoy the large redwood grove. Alice Eastwood called this area "Butterfly Spring" because of the many specimens she found here. To continue the hike, take the Colier trail, which starts 30' east of the Colier Spring sign, and climb uphill along the winter streambed.

3.4 Two junctions #4. Go left up to the highway, then head east 100' to pick up the Lakeview trail which climbs toward Middle Peak.

3.6 Junction. Continue downhill on the Middle Peak FR. Back in 1905, two 300' wooden towers, placed on Middle Peak, were reported to be the tallest, wireless telegraph towers in the world. They blew over in a storm in December, 1905 and were not replaced. The current relay towers date from the 1950s. The Water District hopes that someday they can be removed for aesthetic reasons.

4.0 Junction #1. Follow the highway left up to the parking area.

4.3 Back at the parking area with water, tables and restrooms.

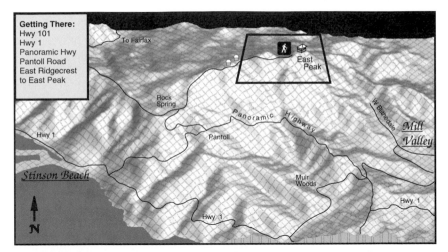

Getting There:
Hwy 101
Hwy 1
Panoramic Hwy
Pantoll Road
East Ridgecrest
to East Peak

To Fairfax

East
Peak

Rock
Spring

Panoramic Highway

Mill
Valley

To Blithedale

Hwy 1

Pantoll

Stinson Beach

Muir
Woods

Hwy 1

Hwy 1

N

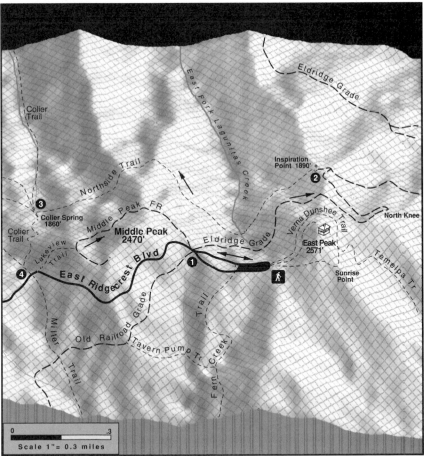

Colier
Trail

Eldridge Grade

East Fork Lagunitas Creek

Northside Trail

Inspiration
Point 1890'

②

③

Colier Spring
1860'

Middle Peak FR

North Knee

Colier
Trail

Middle Peak
2470'

Eldridge Grade

Verna Dunshee Trail

East Peak
2571'

Lakeview Trail

East Ridgecrest Blvd

①

Temelpa Tr.

④

Sunrise
Point

Miller Trail

Old Railroad Grade

Tavern Pump Tr.

Fern Creek Trail

0   .3
Scale 1"= 0.3 miles

48

22 Phoenix Lake Trail

Distance: 2.8 miles   Shaded: 70%
Elevation Change: 200'
Rating: Hiking - 8   Running - 9   Bicycle traffic.
When to Go: Best in March and April for water runoff and flowers.

This heavily traveled trail around the lake passes through a mixture of oak, bay and redwood trees with wildflowers and good views.

0.0 Start at Natalie Greene Park in Ross. Notice the massive slide that occurred in 1986. Slide debris has raised this area by 3' as can be seen by the partially buried telephone booth in the center of the parking area. Take the trail up the left side of the creek to the dam.

0.2 Dam. Go left to circle the lake clockwise. The milky-green color of the water is due to algae and sediment, which are removed when the water is treated. However, this lake is so small that its water is only used for drinking during drought years.

0.8 Junction #1. Turn right and take the signed Gertrude Ord trail up the stairs. The trail passes through a mixture of tall oak, bay, Douglas fir and madrone trees shading low-growing tanoak and fuzzy-leafed hazel. Pink trillium, white milkmaids and blue hound's tongue can be found in February and March.

1.3 Junction. The stairs down to the right can be used as a shortcut in dry times. For a more interesting route, follow the trail left into the redwood ravine. The storm of 1986 scoured the creek bottom lowering the channel by three feet. Upstream, previous mudslides have left much debris including several large trees.

2.0 Junction #2. Turn right at the small bridge to take the Phoenix Lake Rd east towards the dam. Up ahead, Phoenix Log Cabin, built in 1893 for the Porteous Ranch foreman, has been restored. Notice the octagonal turret and natural window frames. The cabin is not open to the public. Please do not enter the area, as it is also a ranger residence.

Phoenix Log Cabin
Originally Built in 1893

2.5 Dam. Go left down the road.

2.8 Parking area with water, tables and restrooms facilities.

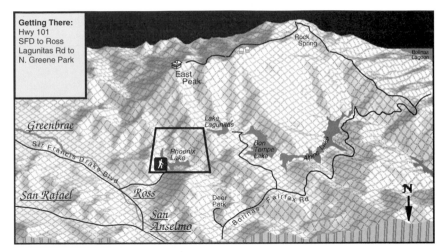

Getting There:
Hwy 101
SFD to Ross
Lagunitas Rd to
N. Greene Park

Rock
Spring

Bolinas
Lagoon

East
Peak

Greenbrae

Lake
Lagunitas

Sir Francis Drake Blvd

Phoenix
Lake

Bon
Tempe
Lake

Alpine Lake

San Rafael *Ross*

Deer
Park

Fairfax Rd

*San
Anselmo*

Bolinas

N

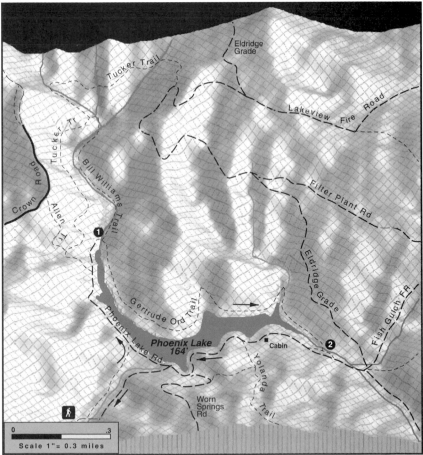

Eldridge
Grade

Tucker Trail

Lakeview Fire Road

Tucker Tr

Crown

Road

Bill Williams Trail

Allen Tr

Filter Plant Rd

Eldridge Grade

Fish Gulch FR.

❶

Gertrude Ord Trail

Phoenix Lake Rd

**Phoenix Lake
164'**

Cabin

❷

Yolanda Trail

Worn
Springs
Rd

0   .3
Scale 1"= 0.3 miles

50

23 Tucker - Bill Williams Trails

Distance: 2.9 miles   Shaded: 80%
Elevation Change: 400'   One short, steep section.
Rating: Hiking - 8   Running - 9
When to Go: Good anytime, best after rain.

This is a fine hike that explores two small canyons offering enchanting oak-bay woods, redwoods, ferns and mosses in a creekside setting.

0.0 Start at Natalie Greene Park in Ross. From the parking lot, take the trail up the left side of the creek to the stairs and dam.

0.2 Dam. Go left to circle the lake clockwise. Ahead, look for seasonal wildflowers: red Indian warrior in March, white iris in April, blue brodiaea in May and red clarkia in June.

0.6 Junction #1. Turn left on the signed Harry Allen trail and head into a small ravine with oak, bay and buckeye trees. Early flowers include pink shooting star, blue hound's tongue, and white zigadene. Later flowers include white modesty, blue dicks and wood rose.

0.8 Junction. The Harry Allen trail goes left uphill. Stay right and follow the Tucker trail past mosses, lichens and maidenhair ferns. Several small deer paths cross the trail before the next junction.

1.1 Main canyon. Redwoods grow along the north slope of Bill Williams canyon. Oaks and bays grow here along the south side. Up ahead, a small dam is just visible down the steep hillside.

Maidenhair Fern

1.5 Two junctions #2. An unmaintained trail comes down from the left. At the second junction, 100' ahead, turn right and go steeply down to the creek on the Bill Williams trail.

1.6 Two bridges. The trail makes three crossings of the creek: two by bridge and one by foot. (The creek may not be fordable in high water.) Cross the first bridge, go uphill 100' to a junction, turn right and go down to the creek for the second crossing over rocks. Continue along the creek past the dam to the second bridge. This dam was built in 1886 as part of a local water supply before Phoenix Lake was created in 1906. Cross the creek and continue through the redwoods.

2.1 Phoenix Lake Rd. Continue along the lake to the dam.

2.6 Dam and junction. Cross the dam and take the road downhill.

2.9 Back at the parking area with water, tables and restrooms.

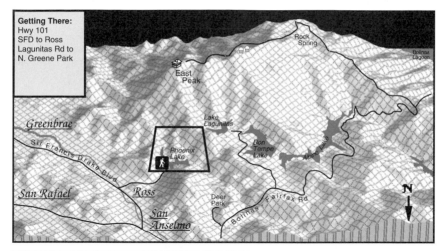

Getting There:
Hwy 101
SFD to Ross
Lagunitas Rd to
N. Greene Park

Greenbrae

Sir Francis Drake Blvd

San Rafael

Ross

San Anselmo

East Peak

Rock Spring

Bolinas Lagoon

Lake Lagunitas

Phoenix Lake

Bon Tempe Lake

Alpine Lake

Deer Park

Bolinas - Fairfax Rd

N

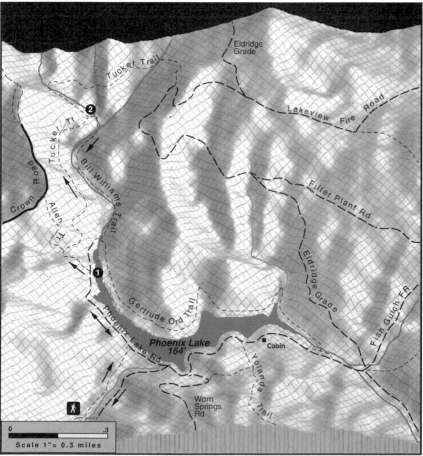

Eldridge Grade

Tucker Trail

Lakeview Fire Road

Tucker Tr

❷

Crown Road

Tucker Tr

Allen Tr

Bill Williams Trail

Filter Plant Rd

Eldridge Grade

❶

Gertrude Ord Trail

Fish Gulch FR

Phoenix Lake Rd

Phoenix Lake
164'

Cabin

Yolanda Trail

Worn Springs Rd

0   .3
Scale 1"= 0.3 miles

52

24 Worn Springs Road to Bald Hill

Distance: 3.9 miles   Shaded: 50%
Elevation Change: 1100'   Steep in places.
Rating: Hiking - 7   Running - 7   Some bicycles.
When to Go: Good any cool, clear, windless day; best in spring.

Take binoculars and water to make the long climb up the road to Bald Hill. Spectacular views and good wildflowers in spring.

0.0 Start at Natalie Greene Park in Ross. From the parking lot, take the road uphill past oak, bay and madrone. Look for white wild onion and iris along the road in spring.

0.3 Dam. Take the Phoenix Lake Rd to the right.

0.4 Junction #1. Take the signed Worn Springs Rd right toward Bald Hill. This road was named after George Austin Worn, descendant of the family that founded the town of Ross.

0.7 Reservoir and junction. The small Ross Reservoir can hold one million gallons and is only used during drought. Take the left road and climb steeply.

1.4 Views. Good views south and east. Yellow buttercup, poppy, white popcorn flower, blue-eyed grass, blue dicks, lupine, and pink checkerbloom grow along the road from March to May.

2.1 Junction #2. The road left is the way down. For now, take the right road 150' to the top of the hill.

2.2 Bald Hill. Spectacular 360 degree views. Explore the hilltop to discover the best wildflower display, often yellow gold fields. To continue the hike, backtrack to the junction and bear right.

2.4 Junction #3. Bear right to head east. There is a good selection of wildflowers 100' uphill from this junction. Down the road, coyote brush and poison oak indicate the coastal scrub community.

2.5 Oaks. Look for two different oaks nearby. The deciduous California black oak has deeply lobed leaves, 3-4 inches long. The evergreen, coast live oak has one inch leaves with sharp spiny edges.

2.9 Gate. Take the paved road downhill past large estates.

3.2 Junction. Take Upper Rd right to Glenwood then right again.

3.6 Junction #4. Take Lagunitas Rd right towards the park. Once past the park gate, look for blue forget-me-nots, white milkmaids, modesty, woodland star and mission bells in early spring.

3.9 Back at the parking area with water, tables and restrooms.

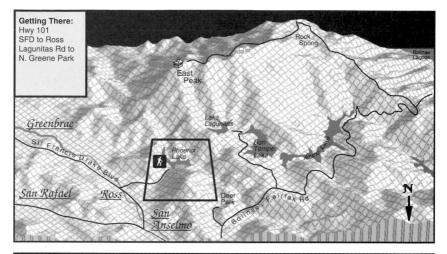

Getting There:
Hwy 101
SFD to Ross
Lagunitas Rd to
N. Greene Park

East Peak

Greenbrae

Rock Spring

Bolinas Lagoon

Lake Lagunitas

Phoenix Lake

Bon Tempe Lake

Alpine Lake

San Rafael   *Ross*

San Anselmo

Deer Park

Bolinas - Fairfax Rd

Sir Francis Drake Blvd

N

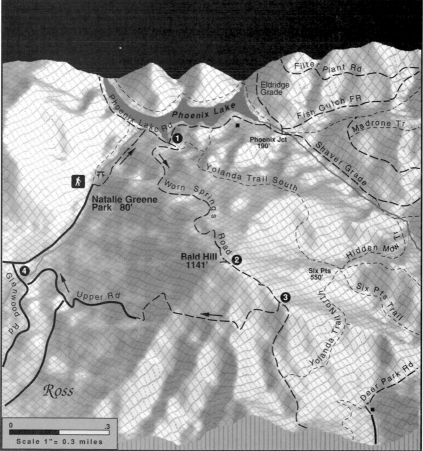

Filter Plant Rd

Eldridge Grade

Fish Gulch FR

Phoenix Lake

Phoenix Lake Rd

Madrone Tr

❶

Phoenix Jct 190'

Shaver Grade

Yolanda Trail South

Worn Springs Road

Natalie Greene Park 80'

Bald Hill 1141'

❷

Hidden Mdw

Six Pts 550'

Six Pts Trail

❸

❹

Upper Rd

Glenwood Rd

Yolanda Trail

N. UP

Deer Park Rd

Ross

0   .3
Scale 1"= 0.3 miles

54

25 Hidden Meadow - Yolanda Trails

Distance: 3.9 miles   Shaded: 70%
Elevation Change: 600'
Rating: Hiking - 9   Running - 8   Part may be overgrown.
When to Go: Good in spring, best in April and May.

The hike explores a small hidden meadow, then climbs steeply to skirt a south-facing hillside with great views and good wildflowers.

0.0 From the Natalie Greene Park in Ross, start out on the left side of the creek. The trail passes through the picnic area, then climbs steeply up to the dam under a dense canopy of bay trees.

0.2 Stairs, dam and lake. Go right on the road across the spillway and circle the lake. Watch for osprey, cormorants and ducks. The cormorants are skillful fish catchers and unwelcome by fishermen.

0.6 Junction, cabin and gate. Continue around the lake. Two hundred feet ahead, Phoenix Log Cabin, built in 1893, has been restored.

0.9 Phoenix Jct #1. Take signed Shaver Grade to the right up towards Five Corners. Shaver Grade was originally a logging road built by Isaac Shaver in the 1890s to haul lumber from near Alpine Dam to Ross Landing (now the site of College of Marin, Kentfield).

1.2 Junction #2. Take the Hidden Meadow trail right along the creek.

1.4 Creek bed, junction and meadow. A large oak, backed by a buckeye welcomes visitors to Hidden Meadow. Stay to the right and continue along a small seasonal creek. Ahead, the trail climbs more steeply on the grassy hillside. Look for yellow buttercups, blue brodiaea and white popcorn flower in April.

1.9 Six Points Jct #3. Take the signed Yolanda trail south towards Phoenix Lake. Colorful wildflowers and spectacular views lie ahead as the trail winds along the south-facing canyon hillside.

2.3 Rock slide. A small rock slide caused by one of the many winter storms. Two hundred feet above the slide is Rocky View Point.

2.4 Wildflowers. Pink shooting stars, blue dicks, yellow poppies, red larkspur and iris stand guard on small rocky outcroppings.

2.7 Spectacular views of Mt Tamalpais!

3.0 Downhill. The trail tumbles downhill past several fallen trees. Stay right at the small Y-junction ahead.

3.2 Junction. Go left on Phoenix Lake Rd towards the dam.

3.9 Back at the parking lot with tables, water and restrooms.

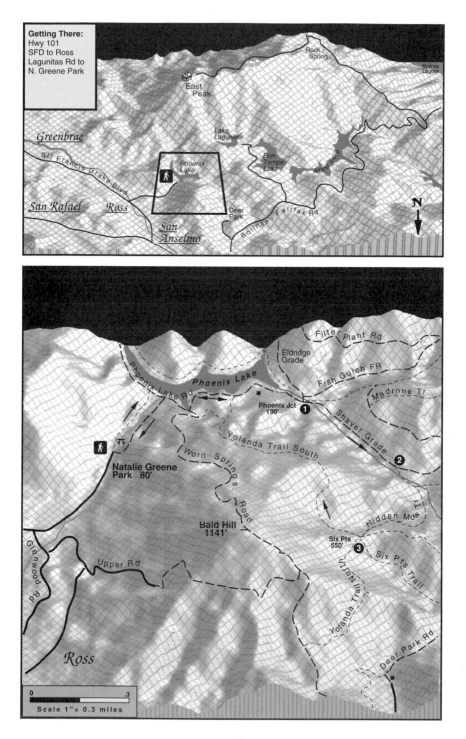

Getting There:
Hwy 101
SFD to Ross
Lagunitas Rd to
N. Greene Park

Rock
Spring

Bolinas
Lagoon

East
Peak

Greenbrae

Lake
Lagunitas

Bon
Tempe
Lake

Alpine Lake

Sir Francis Drake Blvd

Phoenix
Lake

San Rafael   *Ross*

Deer
Park

Fairfax Rd

*San
Anselmo*

Bolinas

N

Filter Plant Rd

Eldridge
Grade

Phoenix Lake

Fish Gulch FR

Phoenix Lake Rd

Madrone Tr

Phoenix Jct
190'   **1**

Shaver Grade

2

Yolanda Trail South

TH

Worn Springs Road

Natalie Greene
Park 80'

Hidden Mdw

Six Pts
550' **3**   Six Pts Trail

Bald Hill
1141'

Glenwood Rd

Upper Rd

Yolanda Trail

Deer Park Rd

Ross

0   .3
Scale 1" = 0.3 miles

56

26 Eldridge Grade - Tucker Trails

Distance: 4.9 miles   Shaded: 60%
Elevation Change: 600'   Steep in places.
Rating: Hiking - 9   Running - 8   Bicycles on weekends.
When to Go: Best in late winter and early spring.
Lots of water, views and wildflowers make this a great hike on the steep north slope of Mt Tam. May be impassable after heavy rain.

0.0 Start at Natalie Greene Park in Ross. From the parking lot, take the road uphill past oak, bay and madrone. Watch out for poison oak.

0.3 Dam. Go right. In April, look for pink Chinese houses.

0.9 Phoenix Jct #1. Take the first left road, signed Eldridge Grade, for a steady climb through an interesting combination of redwood, big-leaf maple, oak, bay and madrone.

This road was built as a toll road by John C. Eldridge in the 1880s as the first wagon road to the summit. It has suffered many slides and is now being maintained as a trail. It is a heavily traveled bicycle route.

1.6 Rock garden. In an open ravine, water streams down large rocks to nourish mosses, lichens and spring flowers including red larkspur.

1.7 Junction with Filter Plant Rd. Continue left uphill.

2.1 Hairpin junction. Take either road as they merge ahead.

2.5 Junction #2 with the Tucker trail. As the road curves right, take the signed Tucker trail left towards Phoenix Lake.

3.0 Creek. The trail makes a steep descent down the north slope of Mt Tam past tumbling creeks, cascading waterfalls, western azalea, redwood and iris. This is a magnificent section of trail.

3.4 Bill Williams Creek. Cross the creek to head uphill.

3.5 Junction #3. Take the signed Bill Williams trail left, steeply downhill to the bridge.

3.6 Two bridges. The trail makes three crossings of the creek: two by bridge and one by foot. Cross the first bridge, go uphill 100 feet to a junction, turn right and go down to the creek for the second crossing by rocks. Walk along the creek past the dam to the second bridge. Cross the creek again and continue along the redwood trail.

4.1 Phoenix Lake Rd. Continue right around the lake.

4.6 Dam. Before the dam, go right on the trail, then down the stairs.

4.9 Back at the parking lot with tables, water and restrooms.

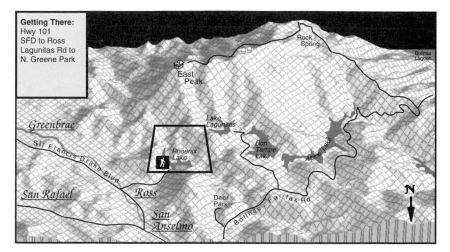

Getting There:
Hwy 101
SFD to Ross
Lagunitas Rd to
N. Greene Park

Rock Spring

Bolinas Lagoon

East Peak

Lake Lagunitas

Greenbrae

Bon Tempe Lake

Alpine Lake

Sir Francis Drake Blvd

Phoenix Lake

San Rafael

Ross

Deer Park

Fairfax Rd

San Anselmo

Bolinas

N

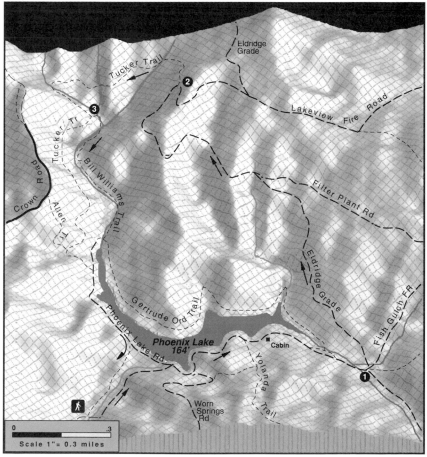

Eldridge Grade

Tucker Trail

❷

❸

Lakeview Fire Road

Tucker Tr

Crown Road

Allen Tr

Bill Williams Trail

Filter Plant Rd

Eldridge Grade

Gertrude Ord Trail

Fish Gulch FR

Cabin

Phoenix Lake 164'

Phoenix Lake Rd

Yolanda Trail

❶

Worn Springs Rd

0   .3

Scale 1"= 0.3 miles

27 Phoenix Lake to East Peak

Distance: 11.7 miles   Shaded: 50%
Elevation Change: 2600'   Steep and rocky in places.
Rating: Hiking - 7   Running - 6   Heavy bicycle traffic at times.
When to Go: Best when cool and clear.

This long and strenuous hike to the top of Mt Tamalpais offers incomparable views in all directions.

0.0 Start at Natalie Greene Park in Ross. From the parking lot, take the trail up the left side of the creek to the stairs and dam.

0.2 Junction and dam. Take the road left around the lake.

0.6 Junction #1. Take the signed Harry Allen trail left uphill.

0.8 Junction with the Tucker trail. Just past the creek, continue left on the Harry Allen trail and head up a steep rocky path.

1.0 Paved street, houses and street junction. Head right on Crown Rd. Up ahead, at the street junction, continue straight on Phoenix Rd.

1.2 Three junctions. Bear left at the Y in the street to the signed trailhead. Then take the right trail, the Kent FR, which is overgrown with broom for 100 yds before entering a redwood forest.

1.6 Junction #2. Take the Indian FR left, which heads steeply uphill, but provides great views across Bill Williams canyon to Mt Tam.

2.0 Junction with Blithedale Ridge FR. Continue climbing. Up ahead, the trail enters the north-facing shadow of East Peak.

2.5 Junction #3. Take Eldridge Grade left. This road was built for wagon traffic in the late 1880s, so it climbs gradually.

3.1 Junction with Wheeler trail. This southern-most section of Eldridge offers great views south to San Francisco and the coast.

3.7 Inspiration Point. A rocky outcropping provides a rest stop and views north. You have to scramble around the rocks to climb them.

4.9 Ridgecrest Blvd and junction #4. Take the paved road east.

5.1 East Peak Visitor Center. More great views, water, restrooms and picnic area. When done retrace your steps to Eldridge Grade.

5.3 Eldridge Grade. Take the road downhill to the Tucker trail.

9.2 Junction #5. Take the Tucker trail right which enters a ravine.

10.9 Junction with Harry Allen trail. Continue straight downhill to the lake and junction #1, then head right on the Phoenix Lake Rd.

11.7 Back at the parking area with restrooms and water.

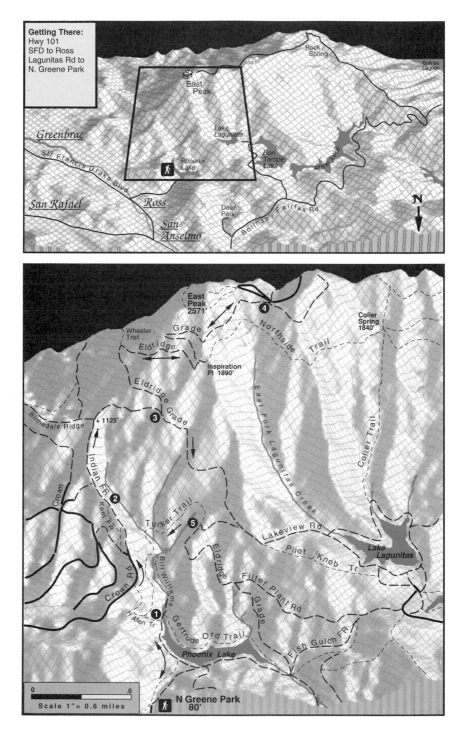

Getting There:
Hwy 101
SFD to Ross
Lagunitas Rd to
N. Greene Park

Rock
Spring

Bolinas
Lagoon

East
Peak

Lake
Lagunitas

Greenbrae

Sir Francis Drake Blvd

Bon
Tempe
Lake

Alpine Lake

Phoenix
Lake

San Rafael

Ross

San
Anselmo

Deer
Park

Fairfax Rd

Bolinas

N

East
Peak
2571'

④

Collier
Spring
1840'

Wheeler
Trail

Grade

Northside   Trail

Eldridge

Inspiration
Pt 1890'

Eldridge Grade

Blithedale Ridge

+1125'

③

East Fork Lagunitas Creek

Collier Trail

Crown

Indian FR

Kent FR

②

Tucker Trail

⑤

Lakeview Rd

Pilot   Knob   Tr

Lake
Lagunitas

Crown Rd

Bill Williams

Eldridge

Filter Plant Rd

Grade

Fish Gulch FR

H Allen Tr

①

Gertrude

Ord Trail

Phoenix Lake

0   .6
Scale 1"= 0.6 miles

N Greene Park
80'

60

28 Deer Park Rd - Yolanda Trail

Distance: 3.3 miles   Shaded: 70%
Elevation Change: 400'   Steep in places.
Rating: Hiking - 9   Running - 8   Some bicycle traffic.
When to Go: Good November to May, best in April for iris.

This is a good wildflower hike that begins in a canyon, then climbs the north slopes of Bald Hill. Great views of Mt Tam and Bolinas Ridge.

0.0 Start at Deer Park in Fairfax. From the parking area, go left around the school and cross the field. Deer Park Rd begins at the gate just past a magnificent bay tree and heads into a canyon.

0.5 Oak Tree Jct #1. Take the narrow Junction trail right past French broom. Then cross a small bridge and climb up an open hillside. Look for blue dicks, buttercup, filaree, paintbrush, clover, lupine, monkeyflower and popcorn flower scattered on the hillside in spring.

0.9 Boy Scout Jct. Take the Bald Hill trail which starts up on a steep, rutted path. About 100' up from the junction, at the end of the rutted section, look for a view west, framed by trees, to Bolinas Ridge. Below the ridge, you can see the Bolinas-Fairfax Rd. In 1884, it was a stagecoach road to Bolinas, once Marin's largest town as loggers provided lumber for San Francisco.

1.3 Junction. Continue left on the Bald Hill trail. Up ahead, the trail skirts above Hidden Meadow and offers great views to Mt Tam.

1.6 Six Points Jct #2. Take the signed Yolanda trail (Yolanda North), towards Worn Springs Rd. The narrow trail follows the hillside in and out of wooded stands of oak, bay and madrone.

2.1 Knoll. A spur trail heads 100' onto an oak-covered knoll. Lots of lichen on the trunks.

2.3 Wildflowers. Another open hillside displays spring flowers including white woodland star, baby blue-eyes and in late April, Chinese houses.

2.5 Junction with Worn Springs Rd. Turn left and head downhill. Good views east to the bay.

Chinese Houses

2.9 Junction #3. Follow the signed Deer Park trail left as it descends in switchbacks down the hillside. Lots of wildflowers bloom here in early spring, followed later by the sweet-smelling buckeye tree in May. At the bottom of the hill, bear right towards the schoolyard.

3.3 Parking area with water, picnic tables and restrooms.

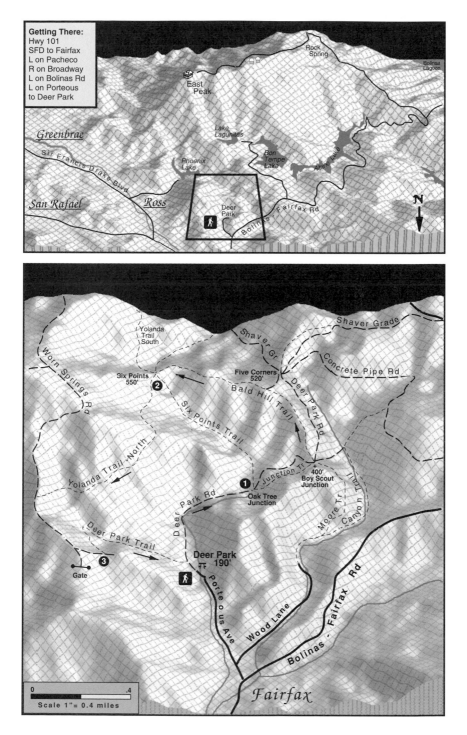

Getting There:
Hwy 101
SFD to Fairfax
L on Pacheco
R on Broadway
L on Bolinas Rd
L on Porteous
to Deer Park

N

Greenbrae

San Rafael   Ross

Sir Francis Drake Blvd

East Peak

Rock Spring

Bolinas Lagoon

Lake Lagunitas

Phoenix Lake

Bon Tempe Lake

Alpine Lake

Deer Park

Bolinas - Fairfax Rd

Worn Springs Rd

Yolanda Trail South

Shaver Gr.

Shaver Grade

Six Points 550'

Five Corners 520'

Concrete Pipe Rd

Bald Hill Trail

Six Points Trail

Deer Park Rd

Yolanda Trail North

Junction Tr.

400' Boy Scout Junction

Oak Tree Junction

Moore Tr.

Canyon Trail

Deer Park Rd

Deer Park Trail

Gate

Deer Park 190'

Porteous Ave

Wood Lane

Bolinas - Fairfax Rd

Fairfax

0   .4
Scale 1"= 0.4 miles

62

29 Deer Park Rd - Canyon - Six Points

Distance: 3.7 miles   Shaded: 90%
Elevation Change: 550'   Steep in places. Can be muddy.
Rating: Hiking - 9   Running - 8   Heavy bicycle traffic weekends.
When to Go: Good November to May, best February through April.

This is a good wildflower hike that explores the hills and canyons west of Bald Hill offering great views and enchanting forests.

0.0 Start at Deer Park in Fairfax. From the parking area, go left around the school and through the field. Deer Park Rd begins at the gate just past a large bay tree and heads into a broad, shaded canyon with majestic oaks, madrone and buckeye trees. Spring wildflowers along the road include white milkmaids, Solomon's seal, yellow buttercup, blue hound's tongue, forget-me-nots, lupine and iris.

0.5 Oak Tree Jct. #1. Just before the road heads uphill, take the Junction trail right past a large oak and cross a small bridge. The trail climbs above a ravine on an open hillside. In late April, look for a small, white flower called jewel flower or *Streptanthus*.

0.9 Boy Scout Jct. Take the spur road downhill to the right towards the signed Canyon trail. The road can be muddy in winter.

1.0 Junction. At the bottom of the hill, cross the creek and go left on the Canyon trail. The trail enters a dark forest of mostly bay trees covered with moss. Up ahead, the trail makes a steep zig-zag climb.

1.3 Junction #2. Take the Concrete Pipeline Rd left. This road was originally a service road for a concrete water pipe built in 1918 to carry water from Alpine Lake to a pump station. A second steel pipe was added in 1926. The concrete pipe can be seen at the bend up the road. There is an excellent display of wildflowers along the roadbank in April, including iris, blue larkspur, Chinese houses and woodland star.

Blue Larkspur

2.0 Five Corners Jct. Take the second left, a spur road, that climbs steeply up towards Six Pts. At the top of the hill, the trail levels out and provides great views southeast to Mt Tam. Look for iris in April.

2.6 Six Points Jct #3. Take the first left, Six Pts trail, down a narrow path marked by wooden erosion barriers. This trail is also known as the "dark trail", as it descends into a forest of bay trees.

3.2 Oak Tree Jct. Turn right and backtrack along Deer Park Rd.

3.7 Parking area with water, tables and restroom facilities.

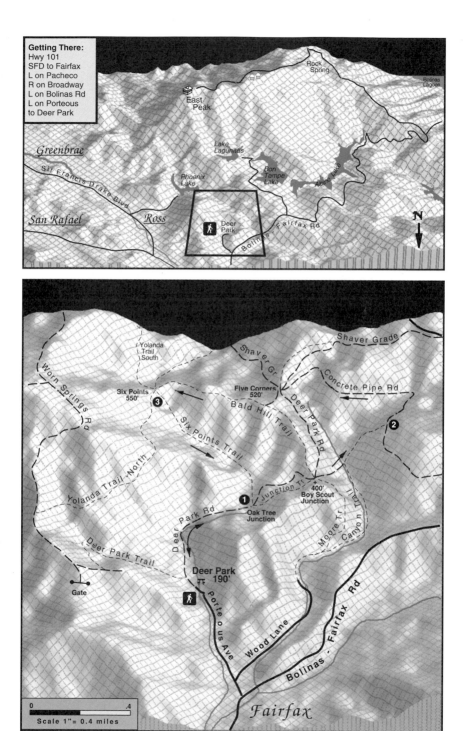

Getting There:
Hwy 101
SFD to Fairfax
L on Pacheco
R on Broadway
L on Bolinas Rd
L on Porteous
to Deer Park

Greenbrae

Sir Francis Drake Blvd

San Rafael   Ross

East Peak

Rock Spring

Bolinas Lagoon

Lake Lagunitas

Phoenix Lake

Bon Tempe Lake

Alpine Lake

Deer Park

Bolinas - Fairfax Rd

N

Worn Springs Rd

Yolanda Trail South

Six Points 550'

Shaver Gr

Shaver Grade

Five Corners 520'

Concrete Pipe Rd

Bald Hill Trail

Deer Park Rd

Six Points Trail

Yolanda Trail - North

Junction Tr.

400'
Boy Scout Junction

Oak Tree Junction

Moore Tr.

Canyon Trail

Deer Park Rd

Deer Park Trail

Gate

Deer Park 190'

Porteous Ave

Wood Lane

Bolinas - Fairfax Rd

Fairfax

0   .4
Scale 1"= 0.4 miles

64

30 Taylor - Concrete Pipe - Bullfrog Rd

Distance: 3.2 miles   Shaded: 60%
Elevation Change: 250'   One short steep section.
Rating: Hiking - 6   Running - 9   Bullfrog Rd can be boggy.
When to Go: Good mosses when wet, flowers in April.

This is a good hike, mostly along fire roads, through open and wooded areas offering a wide selection of wildflowers and local views.

0.0 Start at the parking area just past the Sky Oaks toll booth and walk back towards the toll booth. Notice the large oaks on the right. In the early morning, look for grey foxes that have a den nearby.

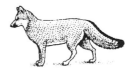
Grey Fox

0.1 Junction. The Taylor trail begins at a gate to the left (north) of the ranger station and starts down parallel to the main road.

0.6 Junction #1 with Concrete Pipe Rd. Bear right and watch for some great spring wildflowers including iris, modesty, blue dicks, Chinese houses, baby-blue eyes, lupine, blue larkspur and pink shooting star. The best display is in late April.

1.3 Five Corners Jct. Take the Elliott trail right to climb the steps and parallel Shaver Grade. The trail gets steep here.

1.6 Junction #2. Go left on Shaver Grade. Watch for bicycles.

1.9 Junction. Go straight across Sky Oaks Rd and take the trail.

2.0 Junction. Take either the dirt road or the parallel trail down towards Alpine Lake. This road was part of the Bolinas - Fairfax - San Rafael stage route that started service around 1890. Look for deer on the open hillside to the right.

2.4 Junction with road to Bon Tempe dam. Continue right.

2.5 Alpine Lake and picnic spot. When full, the scenic lake lives up to its name. To continue the hike, go past the gate along Bullfrog Rd.

2.9 Rock quarry. Red-brown sandstone and blue-green serpentine mark the site of an old quarry along the road. Rock from the quarry was used to build Bon Tempe dam in 1949.

3.0 Junction #3 with golf course road. Keep right. Look for moss and lichen growing on the serpentine rocks breaking through the thin hillside soil. Up ahead, the road may have standing water. If so, you can try to detour to the right towards Sky Oaks Rd.

3.2 Parking area with restrooms and water near the ranger station.

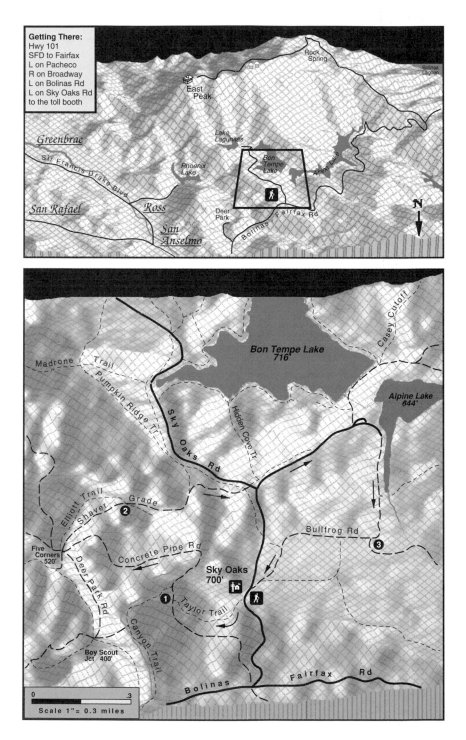

Getting There:
Hwy 101
SFD to Fairfax
L on Pacheco
R on Broadway
L on Bolinas Rd
L on Sky Oaks Rd
to the toll booth

Rock Spring

East Peak

Bolinas Lagoon

Greenbrae

Lake Lagunitas

Bon Tempe Lake

Alpine Lake

Sir Francis Drake Blvd

Phoenix Lake

San Rafael

Ross

Deer Park

Bolinas - Fairfax Rd

San Anselmo

N

Bon Tempe Lake
716'

Madrone   Trail

Casey Cutoff

Alpine Lake
644'

Pumpkin Ridge Tr.

Sky Oaks Rd

Hidden Cove Tr.

Elliott Trail

Shaver   Grade

②

Bullfrog Rd

③

Five Corners
520'

Concrete Pipe Rd

Deer Park Rd

Sky Oaks
700'

①

Taylor Trail

Canyon Trail

Boy Scout
Jct 400'

Bolinas   Fairfax   Rd

0   .3

Scale 1" = 0.3 miles

66

31 Bon Tempe Lake Trail

Distance: 4.1 miles   Shaded: 50%
Elevation Change: 50'
Rating: Hiking - 9   Running - 10
When to Go: Good anytime, best in spring.

This is the best of the three lake hikes. It passes through wooded and open hillsides that provide good wildflowers and great views.

0.0 From the parking area below Bon Tempe dam, head up the dirt road towards the dam, which was built in 1949. At the dam, go right to circle the lake counter-clockwise. Stop and enjoy some great views across Bon Tempe to Mt Tamalpais and also down to Alpine Lake.

0.3 Junction #1 and restroom. At dam's end, take the signed Bon Tempe trail into oak-bay woodland. March flowers include white milkmaids, woodland star, blue hound's tongue and iris.

0.8 Bridge. The first of 3 bridges along the "dark side" of Bon Tempe. Up ahead, many of the taller trees are black oak, too tall to clearly see their distinctive leaves, which are 4-6 inches long with deep lobes. Look for fallen leaves on the path.

1.3 Grassland. Yellow gold fields, buttercup, sun cups, blue lupine and pink shooting star grow among the grasses here.

1.6 Junction #2 and Lagunitas picnic area. Just past the redwood grove, go left across the bridge into the picnic area. Skirt the Lagunitas parking area and continue on around the lake.

2.0 Junction #3. The dirt road heads inland here. Go up 50', then take the trail left. Thirty feet to the right of the junction, notice the large oak and madrone trees locked together in a struggle for sunlight.

2.5 Oaks. Large oaks stand majestically on Pine Point peninsula overlooking the lake. Occasionally, osprey and great blue heron are seen here. Cormorants, gulls and wintering ducks are common.

2.8 Junction with the paved Sky Oaks - Lagunitas Road. Go left. Ahead, the paved ramp provides fishing access for wheelchairs.

3.1 Junction #4. Leave the paved road to follow the trail around the "sunny side" of the lake. Watch for yellow sun cups, buttercup, poppy, white popcorn flower, iris and blue lupine in spring.

3.9 Pumphouse. Follow the road past the pumphouse and up the hill, then head downhill towards the parking area.

4.1 Back at the parking area. Restrooms only.

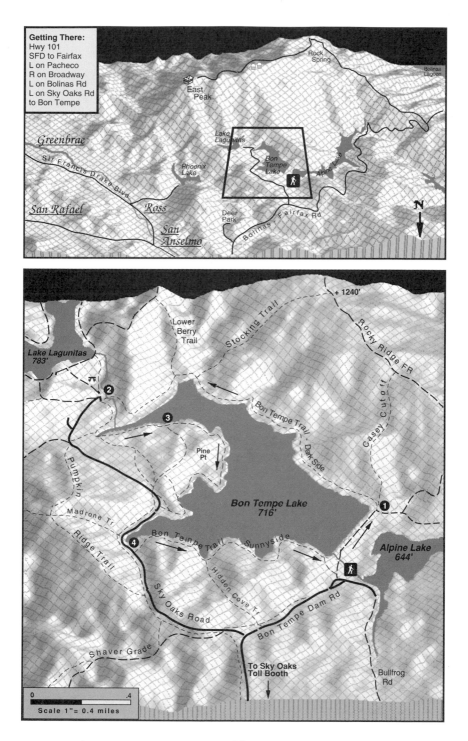

32 Kent Trail - Rocky Ridge Rd

Distance: 5.2 miles   Shaded: 70%
Elevation Change: 500'   Steep and rutted in places.
Rating: Hiking - 10   Running - 6
When to Go: Good anytime, best in spring.

This is an exhilarating hike along the conifer shores of Alpine Lake, up through a redwood forest, emerging onto a ridge with good views.

0.0 Start at the parking area below Bon Tempe dam and head uphill to the spillway. Go across the dam and enjoy the views.

0.3 Junction #1. At dam's end, continue right above Alpine Lake and past lichen-covered oaks. In February, look for white milkmaids, yellow buttercup, pink shooting star and blue hound's tongue among the ferns and mosses along the road bank.

0.8 Pumphouse and Kent trail. The road ends at a pumphouse where water from Alpine Lake is pumped to Bon Tempe Lake and on to a treatment plant. Follow the narrow trail as it winds along the lake through a mixture of chaparral and Douglas fir forest.

1.8 Views. The trail offers great views of conifer forest across the lake like the high Sierra. Just ahead, the trail enters Van Wyck canyon, a gorgeous canyon of tall redwood, bay, ferns and mosses.

2.1 Big fir. A giant Douglas fir stands on a small knoll watching over skinny madrones; its side trunk is as big as the main trunk. Up ahead, the trail enters into a silted canyon with a narrow stream bed.

2.3 Junction #2. Just opposite the sign, Helen Markt Tr, take the Kent trail left uphill past exposed waterpipe. This trail was originally called the Swede George trail after an oldtimer who had a cabin in the area around 1870. Huckleberries can be picked here in early fall.

2.6 Canyon and forest. The trail enters a large canyon covered with tall oaks, bay and redwood. Up past a slide, the trail skirts Foul Pool, then follows the creek through a magnificent redwood forest.

3.1 Junction #3. Take the signed Stocking trail left. The trail heads downhill skirting secluded Hidden Lake, then uphill along a creek bed.

3.8 Junction with Rocky Ridge Rd. Turn left and go up the road 200' for great views south and east. Continue on the road.

4.4 Junction #4. At the far edge of a stand of Douglas fir, look for the Casey Cutoff trail heading to Bon Tempe.

5.2 Back at the parking area. Restroom facilities only.

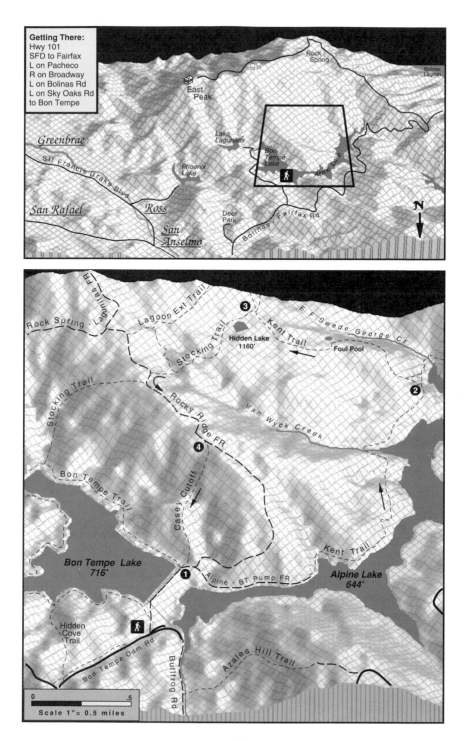

Getting There:
Hwy 101
SFD to Fairfax
L on Pacheco
R on Broadway
L on Bolinas Rd
L on Sky Oaks Rd
to Bon Tempe

Greenbrae

Sir Francis Drake Blvd.

San Rafael

Ross

San Anselmo

East Peak

Rock Spring

Bolinas Lagoon

Lake Lagunitas

Bon Tempe Lake

Alpine Lake

Phoenix Lake

Deer Park

Bolinas - Fairfax Rd

N

Rock Spring - Lagunitas FR

Lagoon Ext Trail

Stocking Trail

Hidden Lake 1160'

Kent Trail

E F Swede George Cr

Foul Pool

❸

❷

Stocking Trail

Rocky Ridge FR

Van Wyck Creek

❹

Bon Tempe Trail

Casey Cutoff

Bon Tempe Lake 716'

❶

Alpine - BT Pump FR

Kent Trail

Alpine Lake 644'

Hidden Cove Trail

Bon Tempe Dam Rd

Bullfrog Rd

Azalea Hill Trail

0   .5
Scale 1"= 0.5 miles

70

33 Lake Lagunitas Rd

Distance: 1.8 miles   Shaded: 70%
Elevation Change: 50'
Rating: Hiking - 9   Running - 10   Bicycle traffic.
When to Go: Good November to May, best February to April.

This is a level hike on roads around the lake with mosses, redwoods, oaks and great views across the lake to Mt Tamalpais. Good birding.

0.0 Start at the Lagunitas parking lot. If you're fortunate, you might hear or see the pileated woodpecker nearby. It is a large 15" woodpecker with a black body, partly white neck and red tufted head. There are many other birds around the lake area, including wintering water birds. Often, you can see osprey flying over the treetops. To start the hike, go into the picnic area and pick up the trail next to the spillway. Climb up to the dam, which was built in 1873.

0.1 Dam. See if you can spot the rare Pacific pond turtles sunning on the floating logs by the dam. Go right over the spillway to circle the lake counter-clockwise. In February, look for white milkmaids, red Indian warrior and blue hound's tongue.

Lagunitas Lake

0.3 Junction #1 with Rock Spring - Lagunitas Road. Continue left.

0.5 Bridge and redwoods. This first of 3 bridges crosses a creek that provides water for a grove of redwoods. You rarely see moss on redwoods, but often can find a grey-green lichen on the bark.

0.9 Mosses. In winter, look for a fine display of mosses, lichens, ferns, succulents and other moisture lovers along the rocky bank.

1.2 Bridge and junction #2. Under a canopy of tall oaks and madrones, the road crosses the East Fork of Lagunitas Creek. Great lichens on the oaks. Bear left at the bridge and again at Lakeview Rd.

1.4 Junction. The road uphill leads to the Pilot Knob trail. Continue left past the large moss-covered oak at the junction.

1.5 Junction. The road veers right up to the ranger's residence. Stay left on the trail as it passes through French broom and down the stairs to the dam. Cross the dam to head down the stairs to the picnic area.

1.8 Parking area. Water, picnic tables and restroom facilities.

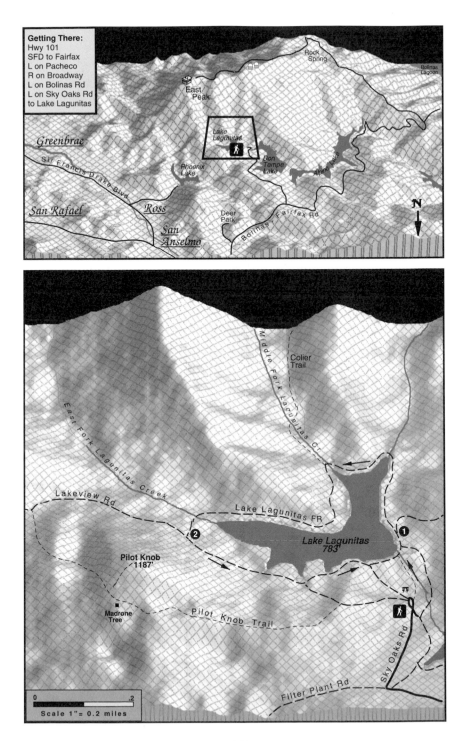

34 Lakeview Road to Pilot Knob

Distance: 2.2 miles   Shaded: 70%
Elevation Change: 500'   One short, moderately steep section.
Rating: Hiking - 8   Running - 9   Some bicycles.
When to Go: Good November to May, best February to April.

This is a good hike through mixed forest, climbing to Pilot Knob for great views, then passing the largest madrone tree seen anywhere.

0.0 Start at the Lagunitas parking lot. Take the road overlooking the picnic area up to the dam. February flowers include white milkmaids and blue hound's tongue under the oak, bay and madrone trees.

0.2 Dam. Look for the rare and endangered Pacific pond turtles that often sun themselves on the floating logs by the dam. Go left up the stairs past the ranger residence and on to Lakeview Rd.

0.6 Junction. The road right goes around the lake. Stay left and enjoy great views to Mt Tamalpais on the right and Pilot Knob on the left.

1.1 Junction #1. Take the signed trail to Pilot Knob left up the hill. The trail climbs steeply through tall madrone, oak, Douglas fir and redwood trees with an understory of tanoak and huckleberry.

1.4 Junction #2. At a knoll, next to a large bay tree, take the spur trail left uphill to Pilot Knob. Ahead, notice the grove of young redwoods that will someday overgrow the tall madrones nearby.

1.5 Pilot Knob at 1217'. Enjoy great views south to Mt Tam, west to Bon Tempe lake, and to Mt Diablo in the east bay. To continue the hike, return down the spur trail and bear left along the main trail.

1.8 Madrone. The grandfather of madrones! An incredible madrone tree with six main trunks, each the size of a single madrone. The tree has limited foliage and may not live many more years. The trail continues along the ridgetop past lichen-covered oaks and more normal-sized madrone trees.

Giant Madrone Tree

2.1 Junction. The road left returns along the lake. Head right past redwood, Douglas fir, oak and madrone trees and follow the steep downhill road back to the parking lot.

2.2 Parking lot. Water, tables, barbecue, map and restrooms.

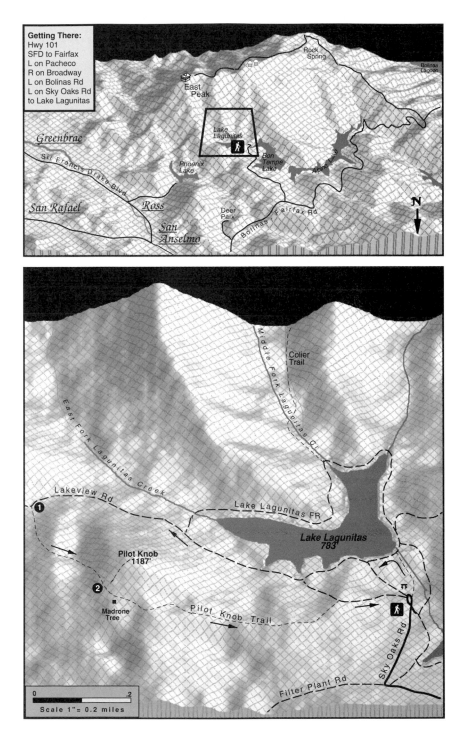

Getting There:
Hwy 101
SFD to Fairfax
L on Pacheco
R on Broadway
L on Bolinas Rd
L on Sky Oaks Rd
to Lake Lagunitas

East Peak

Rock Spring

Bolinas Lagoon

Greenbrae

Sir Francis Drake Blvd

Lake Lagunitas

Phoenix Lake

Bon Tempe Lake

Alpine Lake

San Rafael

Ross

San Anselmo

Deer Park

Bolinas Fairfax Rd

N

Colier Trail

Middle Fork Lagunitas Cr.

East Fork Lagunitas Creek

Lakeview Rd

①

Lake Lagunitas FR

Lake Lagunitas
783'

Pilot Knob
1187'

②

Madrone Tree

Pilot Knob Trail

Sky Oaks Rd

Filter Plant Rd

0 _____ .2
Scale 1" = 0.2 miles

74

35 Pumpkin Ridge - Bon Tempe Trails

Distance: 2.8 miles   Shaded: 50%
Elevation Change: 400'
Rating: Hiking - 9   Running - 7
When to Go: Best around mid-April for spectacular iris.

This hike explores the rolling hills south of Bon Tempe Lake. Good views, oaks and wildflowers lie along the open and wooded ridges.

0.0 Start at the Lagunitas parking lot and head west to the edge of Bon Tempe Lake. Follow the dirt road past the large valves out to Sky Oaks Rd. In spring, look for yellow sun cups, buttercups, blue lupine and a pale purple lily, *Calochortus*, along the open road.

0.2 Junction #1 with Sky Oaks Rd. Cross the paved road and head up the open hillside dotted with lichen-covered oaks. This is classic oak-woodland country with occasional madrones and firs mixed in. The trail follows the ridgetop providing fine vistas of Mt Tamalpais. In April, the ridgetop displays a glorious selection of iris with delicate hues of cream, gold, violet and blue.

Douglas Iris

0.9 Junction #2. Just before the Sky Oaks Rd, take the Sky Oaks-Lagunitas trail right as it parallels the road heading north.

1.2 Junction with Shaver Grade and Sky Oaks Rd. Continue on the trail directly across the paved road.

1.3 Junction #3 with the gravel road to Bon Tempe dam. Go down the road a few feet, then take the Hidden Cove trail left which heads towards a saddle between two tree-covered hilltops. (Power line poles also head for the same saddle.) At the top of the saddle, there is a huge madrone tree 50' to the left (or northeast) of the trail. There are also many non-native Coulter pines, which produce large, dense cones. These trees were planted in the 1930s, but will be removed.

1.6 Junction with the lake. Take the Bon Tempe Lake trail to the left.

1.9 Junction with Sky Oaks Rd. Head right on the paved road.

2.2 Junction. A power pole and garbage can mark this junction. Take the dirt road up and over the small knoll, which offers good views.

2.6 Junction #4. Just before the lake, 50' to the left of the trail, look for a large oak and madrone with trunks entwined. Go left at the lake.

2.8 Parking area with water, tables, barbecue and restrooms.

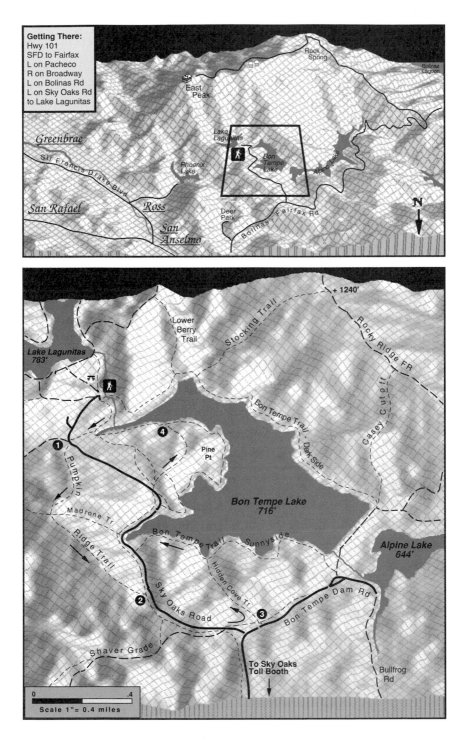

Getting There:
Hwy 101
SFD to Fairfax
L on Pacheco
R on Broadway
L on Bolinas Rd
L on Sky Oaks Rd
to Lake Lagunitas

Rock Spring

Bolinas Lagoon

East Peak

Greenbrae

Lake Lagunitas

Bon Tempe Lake

Sir Francis Drake Blvd

Phoenix Lake

Alpine Lake

San Rafael *Ross*

Deer Park

Bolinas - Fairfax Rd

San Anselmo

N

+ 1240'

Lower Berry Trail

Stocking Trail

Rocky Ridge FR

Lake Lagunitas
783'

Bon Tempe Trail - Dark Side

Casey Cutoff

4

Pine Pt

1

Pumpkin

Madrone Tr

Bon Tempe Lake
716'

Alpine Lake
644'

Ridge Trail

Bon Tempe Trail   *Sunnyside*

Hidden Cove Tr

2

Sky Oaks Road

3

Bon Tempe Dam Rd

Shaver Grade

**To Sky Oaks
Toll Booth**

Bullfrog Rd

0   .4
Scale 1"= 0.4 miles

76

36 Colier - Northside - Lagoon Trails

Distance: 5.2 miles   Shaded: 80%
Elevation Change: 1200'   Very steep and rocky in places.
Rating: Hiking - 9   Running - 4
When to Go: Best in winter for creek flow and in May for flowers.

This strenuous hike, best for experienced hikers, offers cascading creeks, redwoods, views north and a challenge not to get lost.

0.0 Start at the Lagunitas parking lot. Head into the picnic area and along the spillway to the dam. Head right, to circle the lake.

0.5 Bridge and junction #1. Turn right and follow the signed Colier trail up the left side of the creek. Up ahead, the trail crosses the creek twice. Downed trees can make the trail difficult to follow at times.

1.2 Creek junction and crossing. Two creeks come tumbling together here. Fifty yds upstream, cross the creek again and follow the steep trail up and over to the next ridgetop to parallel the new creek.

1.6 Colier Spring at 1840' and a bench for resting. The spring was named after John Monroe Colier, a wealthy but eccentric Scotsman who worked on various trails in the early 1900s. To continue the hike, take the first trail on the right, the Lower Northside trail, downhill.

2.5 Open area, views and junction #2. Take the signed Rocky Ridge fire trail right downhill towards Lake Lagunitas.

2.6 Junction. Go straight across the Rock Spring - Lagunitas FR and take the narrow overgrown trail into the woods. Up ahead, the trail crosses a creekbed and splits. Bear right.

2.8 Junction #3. Take the Lagoon FR downhill to the right.

3.3 Junction and view spot at Serpentine Knoll. Continue on the road, which heads downhill and turns into a narrow, steep and rutted trail.

3.8 Creek and junction #4. After crossing a small creek, the trail enters chaparral and an uncertain junction. Head straight uphill 50', then through overgrown manzanita to the road.

3.9 Junction. Take the Rocky Ridge FR left downhill for 100 yds.

4.0 Clearing and junction. Head right into a large, level clearing on a trail that soon enters the woods. Ahead, the trail gets steep and rocky.

4.5 Junction #5. Take the signed Berry trail downhill.

4.9 Junction with Bon Tempe Lake. Head right along the lake.

5.2 Parking area. Water, picnic tables and restroom facilities.

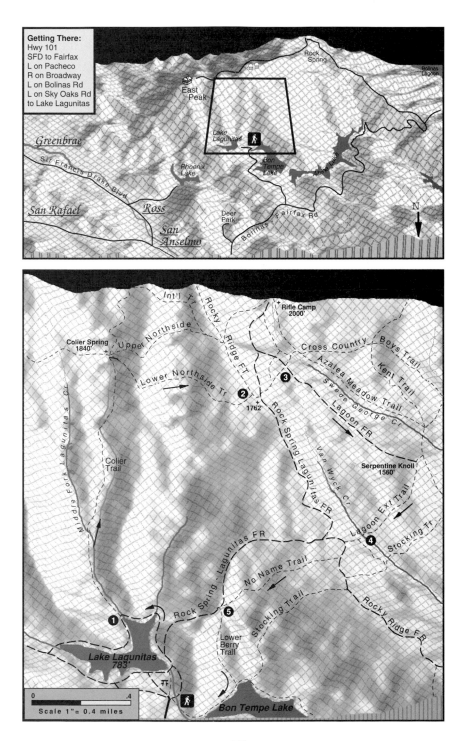

Getting There:
Hwy 101
SFD to Fairfax
L on Pacheco
R on Broadway
L on Bolinas Rd
L on Sky Oaks Rd
to Lake Lagunitas

Greenbrae

Sir Francis Drake Blvd

San Rafael   Ross

San Anselmo

East Peak

Rock Spring

Lake Lagunitas

Phoenix Lake

Bon Tempe Lake

Deer Park

Bolinas - Fairfax Rd

Bolinas Lagoon

N

Int'l Tr

Rocky Ridge FT

Rifle Camp 2000'

Colier Spring 1840'

Upper Northside

Cross Country

Boys Trail

Kent Trail

Lower Northside Tr

Azalea Meadow Trail

Swede George Cr

Lagoon FR

❷

❸

1762'

Rock Spring Lagunitas FR

Van Wyck Cr

Serpentine Knoll 1560'

Lagoon Ext Trail

Colier Trail

Middle Fork Lagunitas Cr

No Name Trail

Stocking Tr

❹

Rock Spring - Lagunitas FR

❺

Stocking Trail

Rocky Ridge FR

❶

Lower Berry Trail

Lake Lagunitas 783'

Bon Tempe Lake

0   .4
Scale 1"= 0.4 miles

78

37 Cataract - High Marsh - Kent Trails

Distance: 7.7 miles   Shaded: 90%
Elevation Change: 2100'   Steep and rocky in places.
Rating: Hiking - 10   Running - 6
When to Go: Best during rainy season and in spring for flowers.

This is a strenuous but spectacular hike in the most remote section of the mountain. Wonderful pools, waterfalls and conifer forests.

0.0 Park anywhere south of Alpine Dam and walk to the signed trailhead 0.2 miles from the dam. The trail starts along the lake in a conifer forest with some bay, oak and big-leaf maple trees.

0.3 Cataract Creek. The trail begins a steep climb up the right side of the creek past refreshing views of pools and waterfalls.

0.6 Bridge and junction. Above the bridge, bear right past a spectacular creekside setting. Ahead, the trail levels somewhat.

1.0 Sunlight. A small open hillside lets in light to grow yellow buttercups and baby blue-eyes. Up ahead, scenery typical of Hawaii.

1.3 Bench and junction #1 with the High Marsh trail. A large, flat bench provides a welcome rest stop. Continue uphill along the creek.

1.5 Laurel Dell picnic area. Tables and restrooms. Backtrack down the trail to junction #1 and take High Marsh trail right, which climbs past a fallen oak tree. Up ahead, on the open hillside, look for woodland star, popcorn flower, fiddleneck, poppy and blue dicks.

3.5 Junction. The Willow trail goes left downhill. Continue right.

3.7 Junction and High Marsh. The CC Boys trail heads right. Stay left to skirt the marsh which is a drainage pond created by a landslide.

3.8 Junction #2. Take the signed Kent trail left downhill.

3.9 Junction near Serpentine Knoll. Bear left and head downhill.

4.3 Junction #3 with the Stocking trail. Take the Kent trail left towards Alpine Lake. The trail descends through an enchanting redwood and tanoak forest, then past a large slide on Swede George Creek.

5.1 Junction #4 with Alpine Lake. Go left as the trail leaves the lake and traverses several ridges. Up ahead, the trail crosses Swede George Creek on a bridge built from lumber floated across the lake.

7.1 Junction and bridge. After a long climb, bear right at this junction to retrace your steps down alongside Cataract Creek.

7.7 Back at the trailhead. No facilities.

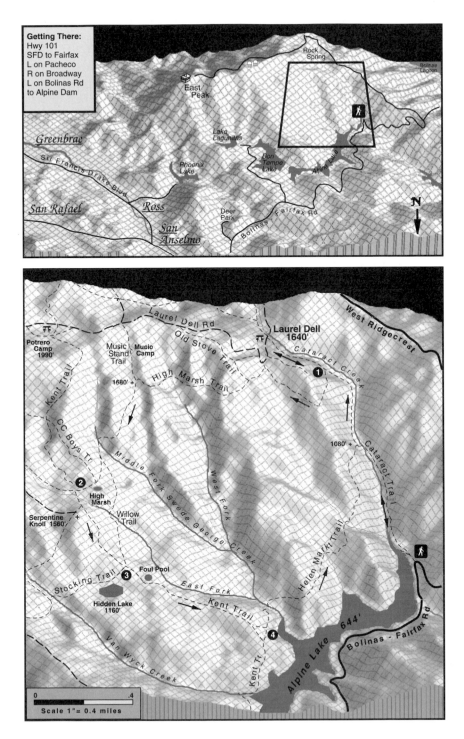

Getting There:
Hwy 101
SFD to Fairfax
L on Pacheco
R on Broadway
L on Bolinas Rd
to Alpine Dam

N

Rock Spring

Bolinas Lagoon

East Peak

Greenbrae

Lake Lagunitas

Phoenix Lake

Bon Tempe Lake

Alpine Lake

Sir Francis Drake Blvd

San Rafael

Ross

San Anselmo

Deer Park

Bolinas

Fairfax Rd

West Ridgecrest

Laurel Dell Rd

Old Stove Trail

Laurel Dell
1640'

Cataract Creek

❶

Potrero Camp
1990'

Music Stand Trail

Music Camp

High Marsh Trail

1680' +

Kent Trail

CC Boys Tr.

Middle Fork Swede George Creek

West Fork

1080' +

Cataract Trail

❷

High Marsh

Serpentine Knoll 1560'

Willow Trail

Helen Markt Trail

Stocking Trail

Foul Pool

❸

East Fork

Kent Trail

Hidden Lake
1160'

❹

Alpine Lake 644'

Bolinas - Fairfax Rd

Van Wyck Creek

Kent Tr.

0 .4
Scale 1" = 0.4 miles

A1 Combination Hikes

The 37 hikes in this book were created to be modular so that it would be easy to combine two or more hikes into hikes of longer distance. Here are just a few possible combinations:

C1 Distance: 9.0 miles   Elevation Change: 1400'
This hike starts at the Mtn Home Inn and explores both sides of the mountain passing by West Point Inn, Mtn Theater and Rock Spring.
0.0 Start at the Mtn Home Inn and follow Hike 10 from mile 0.0 to 2.0
2.0 From West Point Inn, follow Hike 18 from mile 3.4 to 5.2
3.8 From Rock Spring, continue on Hike 18 from mile 0.0 to 3.4
7.2 From West Point Inn, take Hike 10 from mile 2.0 to 3.8
9.0 Back at Mtn Home Inn.

C2 Distance: 9.4 miles   Elevation Change: 1700'
This hike starts at Mtn Home Inn and follows the south side of the mountain all the way to the bottom of Steep Ravine and back.
0.0 Start at the Mtn Home and follow Hike 9 from mile 0.0 to 2.7
2.7 From Alpine Jct, follow Hike 11 backwards from mile 3.4 to 3.0
3.1 From Pantoll, do Hike 14 completely from mile 0.0 to 3.6
6.7 From Pantoll, follow Hike 11 from mile 3.0 to 3.4
7.1 From Alpine Jct, continue Hike 9 from mile 2.7 to 5.0
9.4 Back at Mtn Home Inn.

C3 Distance: 5.0 miles   Elevation Change: 800'
This hike circles the back side of Phoenix Lake, then climbs to Hidden Meadow and Six Points to return via the Yolanda Trail.
0.0 Start at Phoenix Lake and take Hike 22 from mile 0.0 to 2.0
2.0 From Phoenix Jct, follow Hike 25 from mile 0.9 to 1.9
3.0 From Six Points Jct, continue on Hike 25 from mile 1.9 to 3.9
5.0 Back at Phoenix Lake parking.

C4 Distance: 9.5 miles   Elevation Change: 1700'
This hike starts at Lake Lagunitas and climbs to explore the terrain below East Peak, then returns by looping west to Serpentine Knoll.
0.0 Start at Lagunitas Lake and take Hike 36 from mile 0.0 to 1.6
1.6 From Colier Spring, follow Hike 21 from mile 3.1 to 4.3
2.8 From East Peak, continue on Hike 21 from mile 0.0 to 3.1
5.9 From Colier Spring, take Hike 36 from mile 1.6 to 5.2
9.5 Back at Lagunitas Lake parking lot.

A2 A Selection Of Best Trails

Not sure where to go? Here is our selection of best trails to guide you. Remember that the season and weather influence trail conditions.

The 3 Best Creeks and Waterfall Trails
1. Steep Ravine - Hikes 14 or 16
2. Cataract Creek - Hike 37 is best, but also Hikes 17 and 19
3. Redwood Creek - Hike 6

The 3 Best Wildflower Trails
1. Yolanda Trail, both north and south - Hikes 25 and 28
2. Coastal Trail - Hike 15
3. Pumpkin Ridge Trail - Hike 35 or Sun Trail - Hike 5

The 3 Best View Trails
1. Verna Dunshee Trail - Hike 20
2. Old Mine Trail - Hikes 13 and 15
3. A tossup between the Matt Davis Trail - Hike 16, Northside Trail - Hike 18, Bald Hill - Hike 24 and Blithedale Ridge - Hike 1

The 3 Best Running Trails
1. All three lake trails are good - Hikes 22, 31 and 33
2. TCC Trail - Hike 11
3. Troop 80 Trail - Hike 9

The 3 Best Birding Trails
1. Lake Lagunitas Road - Hike 33
2. Simmons Trail - Hike 17
3. Bon Tempe Lake Trail - Hike 31

The 3 Best Flora Trails
1. Steep Ravine - Hike 14
2. Northside Trail - Hike 36 and also hikes 18 and 21
3. Simmons Trail - Hike 17

The 3 Best Beginners Trails
1. Bon Tempe Lake Trail - Hike 31
2. Muir Woods - Fern Creek - Hike 4
3. Phoenix Lake - Hike 22

A3 What Others Say

We asked several veteran Mt Tam people, "What is your favorite hike?" Here is their response:

Wilma Follette
Botanist and hike leader for the California Native Plant Society
"I like the Benstein, Mickey O'Brien and Cataract trails
(Hikes 17, 18 and 19) for spring wildflowers and rare plants."

Jim Furman
Former president of the Tamalpa Runners
"The Matt Davis Extension (Hike 15) and the Old Mine
trail (Hike 13) offer great views."

Ron Angier
Supervising Ranger for Mt Tamalpais State Park
"I like the Bootjack trail (Hikes 6 and 12) as it follows a rocky
streambed through redwood - Douglas fir forest."

Casey May
Chief Ranger for Marin Municipal Water District
"I like the Northside trail (Hikes 18, 21 and 36) for the
panoramic views and varied flora."

Bob Stewart
Hike leader and Naturalist for Marin County Parks
"I enjoy the Sun trail (Hike 5) in early February
to see the first wildflowers."

Meryl Sundove
Hike leader and Naturalist for Marin Audubon Society
"The Lake Lagunitas area (Hike 33) is one of the best
places to see local and migrating birds."

Mia Monroe
Hike leader and Muir Woods Ranger
"My favorite hike is to go down the Panoramic and
Lost trails into Fern Canyon (Hike 7)."

A4 A Trail For All Seasons

December - January
The sun is at its lowest angle of the year and it's often cold and wet. Rainfall averages 20 inches during these two months. But you can beat the indoor blues by getting out and looking for views, creeks, waterfalls, mosses and lichens, and southern exposures. Hikes 1, 2, 7, 8, 9, 12, 14, 16, 17, 19, 23, 26, 36 and 37 are all good choices.

February - March
This is the premier hiking time of the year. Even though rainfall averages 16 inches, the weather is getting better, and water runoff is high. Trillium, milkmaids and hound's tongue start the wildflower parade. All the hikes are at their best, especially Hikes 3, 4, 7, 11, 12, 14, 15, 16, 17, 18, 19, 22, 26, 27, 28, 29, 33, 34 and 37.

April - May
More great hiking time. The weather is at its best, the hills are green and the late wildflowers reach their peak. Be sure to visit the hills around the lakes, when iris peak in April. All the hikes are great, especially Hikes 5, 6, 14, 15, 16, 17, 19, 21, 25, 26, 28, 29, 30, 31, 32, 35 and 36.

June - July
While most of the mountain is hot and dry, Muir Woods and Steep Ravine are often cool and foggy as the Bay Area air-conditioning system runs full blast. Some summer wildflowers, yellow mariposa lily, monkeyflower, poppy, yarrow and clarkia hang on while the hills turn brown. Hikes 3, 4, 14, 17, 19, 32 and 36.

August - September
Now is the time to avoid the dry, dusty roads. Head for the north-facing trails, creeks, conifer forests and ripe huckleberries. Hikes 3, 4, 11, 16 and 32.

October - November
Look for fall red color from poison oak, and yellow and brown colors from big-leaf maple and deciduous oaks. First winter storms arrive. Rainfall, averaging 8 inches during this period, settles the dust and brings out mushrooms. This is great weather time with gusty winds, clear days and marvelous views. It's a good time to head for the coast, south-facing trails and the oak-bay woodlands around the lakes. Hikes 8, 9, 10, 12, 13, 14, 15, 16, 24, 25, 27, 28, 29, 30, 31, 32, 33, 34 and 35.

A5 Geology of Mt Tamalpais

In The Beginning

Several billion years ago, dozens of giant stars formed in our section of the Milky Way Galaxy, lived a short intense life, then died in a cataclysmic explosion called a "supernova". During that explosion, most of the elements heavier than hydrogen and helium were created and spewed forth into the galaxy to be collected and used by later generations of stars, including our sun.

In our solar system, these heavier elements, carbon, oxygen, iron, and radioactive uranium are most noticeable on the inner planets, especially earth. During its early stages, the earth started out with a cool interior and hot surface caused by meteor bombardment. Later, the surface cooled, but the interior heated up due to the slow release of radioactivity by the heaviest of the supernova elements. Today, the earth has a thin crustal surface of rocks floating on a hot molten interior.

Plate Tectonics

The theory of plate tectonics suggests that the earth's surface, the upper 40 miles, is composed of six major rigid plates that move on a plastic interior created by the hot radioactive elements. These plates are constantly interacting as new plate material oozes up in some areas, like Iceland, and old plate material disappears in other areas, like the Aleutians.

The Pacific plate, containing Point Reyes, Los Angeles and most of the Pacific Ocean, is moving northwest relative to the North American plate and is slowly disappearing into the Alaskan trench. Although the Pacific plate is moving at an average speed of 2" per year, the motion is not steady. For example, where the two plates meet, as they do along the San Andreas and related fault lines, there can be sudden plate motions of up to 20 feet as happened in the big San Francisco quake of 1906.

Mt Tamalpais Rocks

Surprisingly, most of Mt Tamalpais is not the result of collisions between the Pacific plate and the North American plate. Geologists believe that Mt Tamalpais was created when the North American plate overrode a pre-Pacific plate between 20 and 60 million years ago. This pre-Pacific plate now lies under the western United States where in the pummelling process of getting there, it produced mountains, volcanoes, hot springs, geysers, and a variety of rock and mineral formations, largely remnants of the old sea floor. The rocks on Mt Tamalpais, along with most of the Bay Area peninsula and mountain rocks, have been named the Franciscan group, after San Francisco.

The most noticeable rocks of the Franciscan group on Mt Tamalpais are sandstones, shale, chert and serpentine.

Sandstone and Shale

Sandstone and shale are sedimentary rocks formed by the erosion and deposit of small particles carried out to sea. Often, plate tectonics will lift sandstone deposits up to form hills and mountains. Sandstone is usually grey, tan or yellow in color depending on the mineral content.

Chert

Chert is a shiny, brittle, quartz rock formed from the skeletal remains of animals raining onto the seafloor where eventually they are heated and crystallized in the presence of a rock called greenstone. Although not common, chert is quite noticeable due to its strong reddish-brown or white coloring and due to its sharp, hard surface that clicks when walked on, sounding like porcelain rubbed together. On Mt Tamalpais, chert outcroppings can be seen on East Peak - Hike 20 and at the bottom of the Taylor Trail - Hike 30.

Serpentine

Serpentine rocks are formed by combining water with the mantel rock, peridotite. Serpentine is usually grey or grey-green in color and some forms have a smooth, soapy feel. Serpentine outcroppings are quite noticeable on both sides of the mountain ridgeline, especially along the Rock Spring, Simmons, Northside and Old Mine trails - Hikes 12, 13, 17 and 21. The seats at the Mtn Theater are serpentine. Rock samples can also be seen in front of the Pantoll ranger station.

Serpentine Flora

Botanists enjoy serpentine areas because it produces unusual plant life. Serpentine soil is high in magnesium and low in calcium, nitrogen and phosphorus. Some plant species, like redwoods, avoid serpentine completely. Other flora, like Sargent cypress and certain species of oak, manzanita and ceanothus only grow on serpentine soils. In general, serpentine soil produces sparse growth or reduced growth and in extreme cases, no flora at all.

A6 Climate of Mt Tamalpais

The earth revolves slowly on its north-south axis like a giant roast in a cosmic barbecue. The sun provides the heat, but the sun heats the earth unevenly with the equatorial regions receiving more energy than the poles. It is this difference in heating coupled with the difference in absorption and release of energy by the atmosphere, oceans and land mass that drives the earth's weather system.

One of the dominant rhythms in this weather system is the jet stream that circles the northern latitudes like a high-flying rollercoaster. In winter, when the jet stream dips down over northern California, it often delivers a series of low pressure storm systems to Mt Tamalpais and brings life-giving rain.

Mt Tamalpais

The climate on Mt Tamalpais consists of warm dry summers and mild wet winters characteristic of the Mediterranean region in Europe. In winter, most of Mt Tamalpais has a uniform climate. January temperatures average 44-46 degrees Fahrenheit while the top of Mt Tamalpais is a little colder and the coastal areas are a little milder. While winter climates are fairly uniform, summer climates offer more variety, creating different climate zones. For this book, we have identified five climate zones.

Zone A - Summer Fogbelt

This climate zone is dominated by the Pacific Ocean and its summertime fog. The zone lies along the coast and up into Frank's Valley and Muir Woods to about 1500'. Exposed areas are often grassland or coastal scrub, while ravines are wooded. Large ravines, created by heavy water runoff, like Steep Ravine and Muir Woods are ideal places for redwoods. These ravines are good places to visit on hot summer days.

Zone B - Summer Windbelt

This climate zone occurs on exposed peaks, ridges, knolls and hills, such as Bolinas Ridge, East Peak and Bald Hill. The conditions that create the summer fogbelt also produce this climate zone. The California central valley gets hot and the hot air rises, drawing in cool ocean air. Strong westerly winds of 25-40 miles per hour roar across these exposed areas almost every afternoon. Because winter erosion of peaks leaves thin soil, usually this zone only supports annual grasses or wind-pruned chaparral.

Zone C - Steep South-Facing Slopes

This climate zone occurs along the steep south-facing slopes of Mt Tamalpais, Bald Hill and other tall hills around the lakes. Summer and winter daytime temperatures are higher here than in surrounding areas. Steep slopes and thin soil usually produce chaparral or grasslands. Wildflowers show up first here. These areas are good places to visit in winter and early spring.

Zone D - Steep North-Facing Slopes

This zone lies along the the steep, north-facing slopes of Mt Tamalpais, and also on Pilot Knob and Bald Hill. Winter sun is almost nonexistent and at higher elevation, summers are cooler. Vegetation, often redwood-Douglas fir forest, is usually more dense as can be seen on the East Peak Loop. The difference between Zone C and Zone D vegetation can also clearly be seen on Bald Hill and Pilot Knob. Wildflowers usually bloom 4-6 weeks later here than in Zone C.

Zone E - Plateau Areas.

This zone occurs around the lakes and in the Rock Spring area. At lower elevations around the lakes, eroded soil has accumulated and supports more tree growth, usually the oak-bay hardwood community. Wildflowers begin in February and March, 2-4 weeks after Zone C.

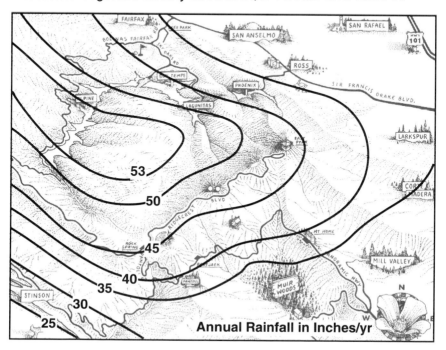

Annual Rainfall in Inches/yr

88

A7 History of Mt Tamalpais

The First People

The last ice age ended about 12,000 years ago, but when it reached its peak, the Pacific Ocean was almost 400 feet lower than it is today. San Francisco Bay did not exist then and Mt Tamalpais was 30 miles from the coast. If Native Americans lived along the Pacific coast or along the great river that flowed past what is now the Golden Gate, the settlements have long been inundated.

It is not known when the first people arrived in the Bay Area. Those who settled in Marin are known as the Coastal Miwok Indians. The oldest known Miwok settlement dates back over 7000 years. There is no record of Indian settlements on Mt Tamalpais itself; it may have been considered sacred. The legend of "The Sleeping Maiden" tells how a young Miwok girl was saved from the devil Diablo tribe by a shuddering of the mountain. Later, her profile could be seen on the mountaintop from a great distance. There are many versions of the legend, most of them created by 19th and 20th century writers.

Wildlife in early Marin and on Mt Tamalpais was much more abundant than it is today. Migrating birds, tule elk, deer, mountain lions and even grizzly bears roamed the land.

The First Europeans

In June of 1579, Francis Drake landed along the Marin coast. Although Drake's party met the Miwoks and might have seen the mountain, what they recorded were "nipping colds as we have never felt before" and "thick mists and most stinking fog." The first recorded name given to the mountain appeared on a map in 1772 where it was referred to as La Sierra de Nuestro Padre de San Francisco. The present name first appeared as "Tamal pais" around 1845. The name appears to come from two similar sounding Miwok words that mean "coast mountain."

It is not certain who the first European climber was; some evidence points to the Englishman Beechey in 1826. By the 1870s many people climbed the mountain as described in the April, 1873, edition of the San Francisco Illustrated Press. "The mountain itself is rugged and rough, but the view from the summit will well repay the toil necessary to get there. Small parties occasionally visit the mountain during the summer months when everything is green, but the character of the trail is such that the majority of them are satisfied with the view from half way up." By the 1890s, the mountain became popular enough for Sidney B. Cushing and others to begin planning for a better way to get to the top.

The Mt Tamalpais and Muir Woods Scenic Railway

On August 26, 1896, seventy-five newspapermen took the ferry from San Francisco to Sausalito, then went by steam train to Mill Valley, to board the Mill Valley and Mt Tamalpais Scenic Railway train for the official grand opening excursion to the top of Mt Tamalpais.

For years, small rugged steam engines carried tourists and travelers up to the famous Double Bowknot at Mesa Station at 1120'. From there, the traveler could continue up to the Tavern of Tamalpais near the summit, or take the Gravity car down into Muir Woods. At West Point Inn, the passenger could get off the train and hike to the Mtn Theater or take the stage coach to Bolinas.

In its heyday, an estimated 50,000 visitors a year rode to the top of

Old Railroad Ad

Mt Tamalpais, many of them enjoying the scenery by hiking back down to Mill Valley. By 1925, the increasingly pervasive influence of the automobile produced talk of converting the railroad bed to a toll road. In 1929, a serious mountain fire dealt the railroad a blow from which it never fully recovered.

Muir Woods National Monument

The redwoods of Muir Woods have been visited by more people than any other redwood grove in the world. Annually, over 1.5 million people discover the grandeur and beauty of these magnificient trees. That this grove of virgin redwoods is still standing today is largely the result of perseverance by one man, William Kent. Around 1900, improved logging methods made it feasible to log what was called Sequoia Canyon. Conservationists persuaded Kent to buy and protect the woods. However, the trees were still not safe. In 1907, a local water company condemned the canyon for use as a reservoir. Kent offered to give the land to the Federal Government, but was refused. Then, he tried to persuade Congress to declare the woods a national park, but it rejected the idea. Finally, President Theodore Roosevelt, using his presidential powers, accepted the land as a National Monument in 1908.

Today, Muir Woods is open for day use from 8 am to sunset. Because of the large number of visitors, camping, picnicking, bicycles and pets are not allowed in the park. There is a visitor center, small snack shop and gift shop near the park entrance. For more information, check at the ranger station, 415-388-2595.

Mount Tamalpais State Park

In 1925, developers began advertising lots for sale on the southern slopes of Mt Tamalpais. Alarmed, the Tamalpais Conservation Club, or TCC, began a campaign to preserve the mountain for public use. The TCC was founded in 1912 and became known as the "Guardian of the Mountain". By 1928 the campaign raised over $30,000 to purchase land and to donate it to the State of California. Later, William Kent, a few hours before his death in 1928, gave another 350 acres to the state that included Steep Ravine and the Mtn Theater. The state park was officially created in 1931.

Today, the park occupies over 6000 acres, mostly on the south side, west side and on the ridgeline of the mountain. The two major visiting areas are East Peak and the Mtn Theater. The theater, long an attraction, held its first play back in 1913. Then, the audience sat and the actors performed on the sloping, grassy hillside of a natural amphitheater. The current theater, built of 40,000 stones, some up to 4000 pounds, was constructed by the Civilian Conservation Corps, or CCC, in the middle 1930s. Over 200 men worked on the theater and on expanding and improving nearby trails. The theater was carefully constructed as a replica of a Greek amphitheater and named for Sidney B. Cushing, one of the founders of the railroad.

Although East Peak and the Mtn Theater are focal points of the park, the hiking trails, views and flora are the main attractions. Over 30 miles of State Park trails connect with GGNRA, Muir Woods and the Water District trails to create a 200 mile hiking wonderland.

Day use of the park begins 1/2 hour before sunrise and ends 1/2 hour after sunset at the gates across Ridgecrest Boulevard. Picnic areas are located at Bootjack, Pantoll and East Peak, but because of extreme summer fire hazards, the East Peak area does not permit fires or stoves. Limited camping is available near the ranger station at Pantoll and a small visitor center is open summer weekends at East Peak. Pets are not allowed on park trails or roads.

For more information about the park or trail information, check at the ranger station at Pantoll, 415-388-2070.

Marin Municipal Water District

The three basic necessities of life are air, water and energy. So it is not surprising to discover that, in early times, over 25 enterprising companies used Mt Tamalpais to collect, store and sell water. Today, there is one water company, the Marin Municipal Water District or MMWD. The MMWD was chartered as a public company in 1912. Since that time, it has bought out all the private companies operating on Mt Tamalpais and now owns about 60% of the area shown on the Mt Tamalpais map. Four of the district's seven reservoirs and their watersheds are located on the immediate north side of the mountain. These are:

Reservoir	Year	Dam Height	Area	Rainfall
Lagunitas	1873	50 feet	23 acres	52 inches
Phoenix	1905	95 feet	25 acres	47 inches
Alpine	1918	140 feet	219 acres	49 inches
Bon Tempe	1948	94 feet	130 acres	43 inches

Rainfall records for Lake Lagunitas go back over 100 years and during that period, the heaviest rainfall season was in 1889/90 when over 112 inches of rain was recorded. The minimum rainfall season occurred in 1923/24 when only 19 inches was recorded. The heaviest monthly rainfall occurred in January, 1896, when 44 inches fell.

The Water District welcomes public use of the watershed with a land policy of "passive use and minimum impact." This policy lets nature take care of the land and vegetation, although fire control, pigs, deer, roads and humans have created some disturbances.

The watershed lands open at 7:00 am in summer and 8:00 am in winter until sunset. Hikers, bikers, horses and runners should stay on designated trails and roads. Pets should be on a leash and fires should be kept in official barbecue pits. Fishing is encouraged and requires possession of a California State fishing license. Swimming or bathing in the lakes is prohibited.

The Water District operates one ranger station on the mountain, located along the Sky Oaks Rd outside of Fairfax. Next to the ranger station is the toll booth where a daily fee is collected for bringing a car into the lakes area. For more information or current trail conditions, check at the ranger station, 415-459-5267.

A8 Animals and Animal Tracks

In the early days before the Europeans came, the San Francisco bay area and Mt Tamalpais were rich in wild life. Among the large animals, there were grizzly and black bear, mountain lions, coyotes, tule elk and deer. The bear are gone, as are the tule elk. The coyotes may be returning, and possibly, one or two mountain lions remain. The only large mammal to continuously inhabit the land is the mule deer.

Mule Deer

The black-tailed or mule deer are abundant on Mt Tamalpais. They are most noticeable on the hills around the lakes and on the coast. Males begin rutting in fall and should be considered dangerous. Antlers are shed in the winter. Females usually give birth to two fawns in the spring. You can almost always spot deer in the early morning and late afternoon on the hills

Mule Deer

north of Bon Tempe dam, Hikes 30 and 31 and along Pumpkin Ridge, Hike 35.

Smaller Animals

There are dozens of smaller animals living on Mt Tamalpais. These include squirrels, chipmunks, possums, shrews, weasels, moles, skunks, jack rabbits, raccoons, rats, feral pigs, bats, foxes and bobcats.

The pigs are non-natives, introduced elsewhere for hunting. In the 1980s, there were as many as 200 wild pigs on the mountain causing considerable damage digging roots and bulbs. By the 1990s, their numbers have been reduced significantly by traps and hunters.

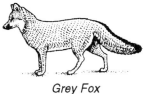

The grey fox can sometimes be seen in oak-bay woodland hills around the lakes and in the coastal grasslands. They often have a reddish hue on the front flanks and can also be identified by their black-tipped tail.

Grey Fox

Bobcats are common on Mt Tamalpais, but probably seen less often than foxes. They can be found in coastal canyons, oak-woodland hills and along the edges of meadows. They are slightly larger than a domestic cat and are identified by their short ears and stubby tail.

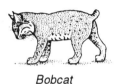

Bobcat

Animal Tracks

Most animals are not easily seen. They are wary of open areas and many only appear at dusk or at night. Their footprints are the primary evidence we see during the daytime.

The first thing to check when looking at animal tracks is the number of toes. Deer and pigs have two toes. Dogs, foxes, cats, bobcats and rabbits have four toes. Raccoons, weasels and skunks have five toes.

Track size depends on several factors, the size and age of the animal, whether it's the front or hind foot, condition of the ground and whether the animal is walking or running. The tracks shown here are about 3/4 actual size for an adult animal.

Grey Fox 1.5-2"

Skunk 1-1.5"

Walking Deer 2-3"

Bobcat 1.5-2"

Running Deer 2-3"

Raccoon 2-4"

94

Oakland Star Tulip
Calochortus umbellatus
Plant height: 3-10 inches
Flower size: 1/2-1 inches
Leaf length: 1 basal leaf 6-14 inches
Season: March - May
Habitat: Chaparral and woodlands

Milkmaids
Cardamine californica
Plant height: 16 inches
Flower size: 1/2 inch
Leaf length: 2 inches
Season: January-March
Habitat: Meadows, fields

Modesty
Whipplea modesta
Plant height: 6-12 inches
Flower size: 1/4 inch
Leaf length: 1/2 -1 inch
Season: March-May
Habitat: Wooded or brushy slopes

Other common white-cream wildflowers are:

Fairy Bells ..... Feb-Jul, 2 feet, white, bell-shaped flowers
Morning Glory ..... Mar-Sept, 2 feet, twining vine, pinkish-white flowers
Pitcher Sage ..... Mar-June, 30 inches tall, bell-shaped white flowers
Yarrow ..... Apr-Sept, 18 inches, fern-like leaves, white flower cluster

Popcorn Flower
Plagiobothrys nothofolvus
Plant height: 8-16 inches
Flower size: 1/4 inch
Leaf length: 1-4 inches
Season: April-May
Habitat: Open grassy slopes and flats

False Solomon's Seal
Smilacina stellata
Plant height: 1-2 feet
Flower size: 1/4 inch
Leaf length: 2-6 inches
Season: February-April
Habitat: Wooded or brushy hills

Woodland Star
Lithophragma affine
Plant height: 8-24 inches
Flower size: 3/4 inch
Leaf length: 1/2-1 1/2 inches
Season: March-May
Habitat: Open, grassy slopes

Zigadene
Zigadenus fremontii
Plant height: 1-2 feet
Flower size: 1/2 inch
Leaf length: 8-24 inches
Season: February-April
Habitat: Wooded or grassy slopes

Buttercup
Ranunculus californicus
Plant height: 8-16 inches
Flower size: 1 inch
Leaf length: 1-1 1/2 inches
Season: February-May
Habitat: Grassland, oak woodland

California Poppy
Eschscholzia californica
Plant height: 8-16 inches
Flower size: 1-2 inches
Leaf length: 1-2 inches
Season: March-October
Habitat: Grassy hills, rocky slopes

Cream Cups
Platystemon californicus
Plant height: 4-12 inches
Flower size: 1-1 1/2 inches
Leaf length: 1-3 inches
Season: March-May
Habitat: Meadows and grassy hills

Other common yellow-orange wildflowers are:

False Lupine ..... Mar-May, 2 feet, yellow pea flower, 3 leaflets
Footsteps of Spring ..... Jan-May, 14 inches, early yellow flower
Yellow Mariposa Lily ..... May-June, 14 inches, 3 yellow petals
Tarweed ..... July-Nov, 18-30", aromatic yellow flower, sticky stem

Gold Fields
Lasthenia californica
Plant height: 8 inches
Flower size: 1 inch
Leaf length: 1/2 -1 inch
Season: March-June
Habitat: Meadows, grassy hills

Bush Monkeyflower
Mimulus aurantiacus
Plant height: 2-5 feet
Flower size: 1 1/2 -2 inches
Leaf length: 1-3 inches
Season: March-August
Habitat: Chaparral

Mules Ears
Wyethia glabra
Plant height: 1-1 1/2 feet
Flower size: 2 1/2 inches
Leaf length: 12-20 inches
Season: March-June
Habitat: Woody or brushy areas

Sun Cup
Camissonia ovata
Plant height: 2-7 inches
Flower size: 1/2-1 inch
Leaf length: 1-6 inches
Season: February-May
Habitat: Grassland

A11 Pink - Red Wildflowers

Chinese Houses
Collinsia heterophylla
Plant height: 8-12 inches
Flower size: 1/2 inch
Leaf length: 1/2-2 inches
Season: April-May
Habitat: Shaded canyons, woodlands

Checkerbloom
Sidalcea malvaeflora
Plant height: 1-2 feet
Flower size: 1 inch
Leaf length: 1 inch
Season: March-May
Habitat: Open grassy hills

Farewell to Spring
Clarkia purpurea ssp. *quadrivulnera*
Plant height: 6-15 inches
Flower size: 1-1 1/2 inches
Leaf length: 1/2 -2 inches
Season: May-August
Habitat: Brushy or grassy slopes

Other common pink-red wildflowers are:

Clintonia ..... Apr-June, 18 inches, shiny leaves, pink flower clusters
Indian Warrior .....Jan-Apr, 10 inches, fern-like leaves, red flowers
Red Larkspur .....Mar-June, 18 inches, red 1-inch flower with spur
Wood Rose ..... May-July, 30 inches, shrub with prickles on branches

Columbine
Aquilegia formosa
Plant height: 1-2 feet
Flower size: 1 inch
Leaf length: 2 inches
Season: April-June
Habitat: Chaparral, oak woodland

Indian Paintbrush
Castilleja subinclusa ssp. *franciscana*
Plant height: 8-16 inches
Flower size: 1-1 1/2 inch
Leaf length: 1-3 inches
Season: March-June
Habitat: Coastal scrub

Shooting Star
Dodecatheon hendersonii
Plant height: 8-16 inches
Flower size: 1 inch
Leaf length: 2-6 inches
Season: February-April
Habitat: Moist slopes

Trillium
Trillium chloropetalum
Plant height: 8-16 inches
Flower size: 2- 4 inches
Leaf length: 3 leaves, 3-6 inches
Season: February -March
Habitat: Redwood forests

Blue Dicks
Dichelostemma capitatum
Plant height: 1-2 feet
Flower size: 1 inch
Leaf length: 6-16 inches
Season: March-June
Habitat: Open or wooded hills

Blue-eyed Grass
Sisyrinchium bellum
Plant height: 6-18 inches
Flower size: 1/2 -1 inch
Leaf length: 4-24 inches
Season: March-May
Habitat: Open grassy hills

Douglas Iris
Iris douglasiana
Plant height: 6-18 inches
Flower size: 2-3 inches
Leaf length: 6-18 inches
Season: March-May
Habitat: Open grassy hills

Other common blue-purple wildflowers are:

Baby Blue Eyes ..... Mar-May, 8 inches, pale-blue, one inch flowers
Brodiaea .....Apr-June, 18 inches, spreading cluster of purple flowers
Forget-me-not ..... Feb-June, 12 inches, clusters of small flowers
Slink Pod .....Jan-Feb, 4 inches, broad spotted leaves, purple flower

Hound's Tongue
Cynoglossum grande
Plant height: 1-3 feet
Flower size: 1/2 inch
Leaf length: 3-6 inches
Season: February-April
Habitat: Moist woods, brushy slopes

Larkspur
Delphinium hesperium
Plant height: 1-2 feet
Flower size: 1 inch with spur
Leaf length: 1-2 inches
Season: April-May
Habitat: Oak woodlands

Lupine
Lupinus nanus
Plant height: 4-20 inches
Flower size: 1 inch
Leaf length: 1/2-1 inches
Season: March-May
Habitat: Grassy hills and fields

Mission Bells
Fritillaria affinis
Plant height: 1-2 feet
Flower size: 1-1 1/2 inches
Leaf length: leaves in whorls, 2-6 inches
Season: January-March
Habitat: Shaded woods, brushy slopes

A13 Chaparral Community

The chaparral community, comprised mostly of chamise, manzanita, ceanothus and oaks, makes up about 25% of the native cover on Mt Tamalpais. The three major conditions favoring chaparral growth over other plant groups are summer drought, thin soil and periodic fires. Chaparral are excellent, drought resistant plants that often have small evergreen leaves with a waxy, shiny or hairy covering to prevent water loss and long roots to tap moisture from surrounding soil.

Chamise - *Adenostoma fasciculatum*

Chamise is the most common shrub of the chaparral community. It is a member of the rose family and ranges in height from 3-10 feet with tiny, needle-like leaves and small white flowers that start blooming in May. In the fall, the flowers dry to a reddish-brown color and give the mountain its characteristic autumn hue. You can easily see this effect by looking up towards East Peak from the Mtn Home Inn.

Manzanita - *Arctostaphylos spp.*

There are five species of manzanita found on Mt Tamalpais and all occur in the chaparral community. They range from 3-10 feet tall with simple, oval-shaped leaves and small, urn-shaped, waxy flowers that start blooming in December. The trunks of manzanita shrubs are very distinctive with a smooth, deep reddish-brown bark, that resembles the madrone tree.

Ceanothus - *Ceanothus spp.*

Six species of *Ceanothus*, or California lilac, are found on Mt Tamalpais and these shrubs range in size from 1-15 feet. They have shiny leaves, often with 3 veins diverging from the base. The fragrant flower clusters vary from white to blue to purple and blooming begins in February.

Oaks - *Quercus spp.*

There are several species of oaks (and some hybrid species) on Mt Tamalpais and four of these are found in the chaparral community. Surprisingly, one of the oaks found in chaparral, the canyon live oak, is the same species that becomes a majestic 50 foot hilltop oak under better conditions. The other oaks found in this community are the leather oak, chaparral oak and scrub oak. The leather oak, *Quercus durata*, is restricted to serpentine areas.

Other Chaparral Plants

Other common chaparral plants include toyon, bush monkeyflower, yerba santa, chaparral pea, huckleberry, tree poppy, poison oak, pitcher sage and Indian paintbrush.

Although the chaparral communities of Mt Tamalpais are healthy, they are decreasing in size, especially at lower elevations. Because there has not been a large fire on the mountain in a long time, oak-bay hardwoods and Douglas fir trees have invaded many chaparral areas where soil and moisture conditions are adequate. This process can be seen on several trails including the TCC Trail - Hike 8, Redwood Trail - Hike 3, and the International Trail - Hike 15. However, deer are chaparral's friend. Deer like to eat hardwood acorns and first-year hardwood and Douglas fir growth.

The largest chaparral stands are located high on the south-facing slopes of Mt Tamalpais and can be seen on the Old Railroad Grade - Hikes 2 and 10, Matt Davis trail - Hike 9, Rock Spring trail - Hike 12, and East Peak Loop - Hike 20. Chaparral on serpentine soil can be seen on the Simmons trail - Hike 17 and Benstein trail - Hike 19.

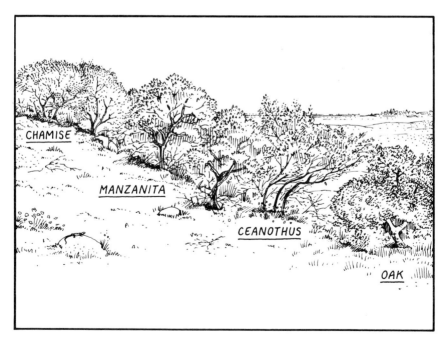

A14 Oak-Bay Hardwood Community

The oak-bay hardwood community, composed primarily of oaks and bay, with some madrone and tanoak, makes up about 25% of Mt Tamalpais flora. This vegetation type is also referred to as the broadleaf evergreen community, in contrast to the needled conifer community of redwood and Douglas fir. However, the hardwood and conifer communities are often found mixed together and this mixture is very common, representing 40% of the vegetation on Mt Tamalpais.

The conditions favoring both the oak-bay hardwood and the mixed hardwood-conifer forest are good winter rainfall and deep soil, required for the development of extensive root systems.

Oak

Several oaks grow on Mt Tamalpais with the coast live oak, *Quercus agrifolia*, the most common. It is a large 30-75 foot tree with a broad round crown and 1-2 inch oval, cup-shaped leaves. The acorns are slender and pointed, and mature in one season.

Other oaks found here include the evergreen canyon live oak (or goldcup oak), chaparral oak and the deciduous California black oak.

Bay

California bay or laurel, *Umbellularia californica*, is companion to the oaks. Its dark green, lance shaped leaves have a distinctive odor when crushed and can be used to flavor beans and stews. The tree is adaptable to most light conditions and is increasing in number, usually at the expense of oaks.

Other Members of the Oak-Bay Hardwood Community

Two fairly common deciduous residents of this community are the big-leaf maple and buckeye. Big-leaf maple are found near creeks and produce a beautiful yellow leaf in fall. Buckeyes are often found in dry ravines and produce clusters of fragrant flowers in May and June,

Two common evergreen members of this community are the madrone, with its distinctive smooth red bark and shiny leaves, and the tanoak. The tanoak ranges in size from a small 3' shrub to a tall 100' tree.

Many shrubs, herbs and grasses are found in the understory of the hardwood forest. These include coffeeberry, California hazel, ocean spray, poison oak, bracken fern and wood rose.

The diversity of plant life in the oak-bay hardwood community leads to a diversity of mammals and birds. It is quite common to see deer, squirrels and jack rabbits. Bobcats and grey fox are present, but harder to find.

Just as the hardwoods invade chaparral, hardwoods themselves can be replaced by Douglas fir under certain conditions. Douglas fir is a natural successor to hardwoods because it grows taller and can shade them out. Bays can be an exception. If bay trees are well established, they form a dense crown that restricts fir seedlings.

Several interrelated factors determine the survival and success of communities: seed production, soil and moisture conditions, light, wind, fires, deer, rodents, insects and birds. For example, oak seeds or acorns, are highly nutritious and have long been a food source for man, deer, rodents and birds. Overpopulation of one or more acorn-eaters can severely limit oak reproduction. In the struggle for success in the hardwood community, bay, tanoak and madrone appear to be increasing, while oaks are decreasing in number.

There are several examples of oak-bay hardwood forest around the lakes - Hikes 22, 31 and 33, along Deer Park Rd - Hikes 28 and 29, on the Old Mine trail - Hike 13 and around Rock Spring - Hikes 17 and 19.

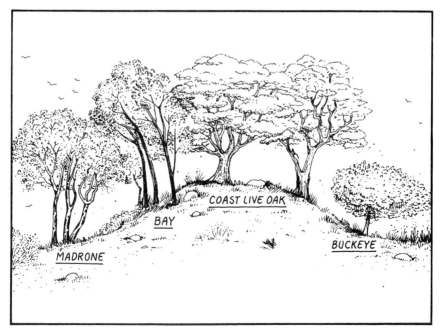

A15 Redwood-Douglas Fir Community

The redwood-Douglas fir conifer community makes up only about 5% of the vegetation on Mt Tamalpais. However, there are many more areas where redwoods and especially Douglas fir have invaded other communities, usually forming a mixed hardwood-conifer community.

Year-round water is the limiting factor in the distribution of these conifers. Winter rains and summer creeks or summer fog are necessary for redwood growth and to a lesser extent, growth of Douglas fir. Summer fog is like summer rain as the fog condenses on the needles high in the crown canopy, then drips to the ground providing up to 20 inches of water per year.

Redwood - *Sequoia sempervirens*

The coastal redwood is the world's tallest tree reaching over 350 feet, although the tallest redwood in Muir Woods stands around 260 feet. Branches of redwoods form flat sprays with dark, shiny green, one inch pointed needles. The cones are small, from 1-2 inches long. Redwoods have a shallow root system spreading out from the base and severe winters will leave a few trees toppled.

Redwoods are fire resistant because of their thick non-resinous bark, moist wood core and because of branch height. The phenols in the bark and wood act as a natural insecticide that discourages insects and consequently limits surrounding bird life. Not only do redwoods form a dense canopy that shades and restricts growth on the forest floor, but also the decomposition of its needles produces a rich humus that favors acid-loving plants like redwood sorrel, trillium, clintonia and several species of ferns.

Douglas Fir - *Pseudotsuga menziesii*

Douglas fir is a conifer and not a true fir tree. Usually, wherever you find redwoods, you will find Douglas fir, only in less moist conditions. Douglas fir grows to heights of 250 feet with a pyramid shaped crown. The one inch needles grow out at any angle and the 2-3 inch cones have mouse-like tails that help distinguish them from redwoods.

Because of hardwood invasion, Douglas fir forests on Mt Tamalpais live in a delicate balance. Parent seed trees start the survival process by scattering seed for the next generation of trees. However, if hardwoods, especially bay trees have invaded the understory, then the Douglas fir seedlings will not get enough light to survive.

Deer help keep the hardwoods in check by nibbling acorns and young sprouts. Fire forms an alternative control of hardwood growth. However, the fire conditions must be just right and often enough to restrict hardwood growth without removing the Douglas fir seed trees.

Other Members of This Community

Tanoak and big-leaf maple are two other trees found searching for light in the conifer forest. In a deeply shaded forest, tanoaks take on the appearance of small shrubs, while under ideal conditions, they can become 100' trees. Big-leaf maple are deciduous trees, which are found near creeks and produce a beautiful yellow-brown leaf in fall.

The redwood-Douglas fir conifer community can be found in three major areas on Mt Tamalpais: Muir Woods - Hikes 3, 4, 5 and 6, Steep Ravine - Hikes 14 and 16, and in the Alpine Lake - Cataract Creek area - Hikes 32 and 37. Small pockets can also be found in ravines on the south side of Mt Tamalpais and around the lakes on north-facing slopes.

A16 Natives Versus Non-Natives

There have been hundreds of non-native species introduced into the San Francisco bay area since the time of the Spanish missionaries. These range from roses to tomatoes to German shepherds to parakeets. Usually, non-native introductions, called escaped exotics or aliens, are not a problem.

Occasionally, non-native introductions do create a problem. For example, the non-native may thrive, reproduce and outcompete native populations. Or, the non-native may bring new diseases or parasites that severely affect local species or damage the habitat. Or, the non-native can cause a population explosion of a native species by reducing or removing a predator.

Examples of Non-Native Invasions

One of the most famous and costliest introductions of a non-native species occurred in Australia in 1859, when a farmer imported a dozen pair of wild rabbits for hunting. Within six years, the population reached 20 million and by the 1930s, the population was estimated at 750 million rabbits. These rabbits devoured crops, fouled water holes and caused soil erosion, consequently reducing the local sheep population by over 50%. It was not until the 1950s that the rabbit population was brought partially under control through the introduction of a viral disease.

There are many, many more examples of destructive alien invasions: starlings, intentionally brought to the United States from Europe in 1890, thrived and replaced several native songbirds. Water hyacinth, intentionally brought in from Central America in 1884, clogged inland waterways and replaced native aquatic vegetation. Mongooses, brought into Hawaii in 1883 to control the rodent population, instead killed the rats natural predators, amphibians and reptiles.

The Japanese beetle was accidentally imported into the United States in 1911 and now defoliates more than 250 species of trees and shrubs. Dutch elm disease was accidentally imported on timber from Europe in the 1930s and will eventually destroy millions of elm trees.

One of the quickest, most costliest invasions in history took place in the late 1980s in the Great Lakes. The zebra mussel, which hitched a ride on a ship from Europe, exploded in numbers, reaching concentrations as high as 700,000 per square meter. These little mussels clogged ten-foot-diameter intake pipes, sunk boats and buoys with their weight and smothered countless numbers of native mussels. Their economic costs may reach as high as two billion dollars annually. Their ecological costs are difficult to measure.

Non-Natives on Mt Tamalpais

The biggest non-native problem on Mt Tamalpais is French broom. It is a member of the legume family that has yellow pea-shaped flowers and bean-like pods. French broom is a drought resistant, evergreen shrub that was introduced for landscaping over 100 years ago. The shrub forms impenetrable thickets that range in height from 6-12'. It reproduces vigorously. In the fall, individual seed pods explode, ejecting up to 300 long-living seeds in a wide circle.

French broom spreads aggressively and can replace many native grasses and shrubs. Its thick cover can shade out and prevent tree seedlings from getting started.

French broom has overgrown parts of the Sun trail - Hike 5, Kent FR - Hike 27, Dipsea trail - Hikes 5 and 14, and Tucker trail, - Hike 23. It crowds many other roads and trails, including the Old Railroad Grade, Phoenix Lake Rd, Shaver Grade and the Pumpkin Ridge trail. French broom has no local predators or diseases to keep it in check. The only known controls are to pull it, cut it or set fire to it.

Other non-native plants that thrive on Mt Tamalpais include Coulter pine, eucalyptus, Monterey pine, acacia, Scotch broom, pampas grass, thistles (yellow star, purple, Russian, bull), fennel, poison hemlock, cotoneaster, gorse, forget-me-nots, oats, Harding grass, Himalaya berry, capeweed, field mustard, wild radish, German ivy, fireweed and vetch. There are other escaped exotics on the mountain, but this is the main list.

The major non-native animal problem on Mt Tamalpais is the feral pig, which numbered over 200 in the 1980s. One pig can do a remarkable amount of damage, digging for roots and bulbs. They have since been significantly reduced using fences and traps, and by hunting.

What You Can Do

If you're concerned about non-native invasions and are interested in doing something about it, here are a few suggestions:

Join the Habitat Restoration Team sponsored by the National Park Service and the GGNRA. Call the Park Volunteer Hotline 415-556-3535 for more information. Join the California Native Plant Society. Team up with local neighbors and clubs for non-native control parties, like broom pulls. Replace non-native plants with native plants in home gardens.

A17 A Quick Guide to Flora

Index of Wildflowers

Baby Blue Eyes ... Mar-May, 8", pale blue 1 inch flowers
Blue Dicks ... Mar-June, 18", blue 1 inch cluster of flowers
Blue-eyed Grass ... Mar-May, 12", blue flower , yellow center
Brodiaea ... Apr-June, 18", spreading cluster of purple flowers
Buttercup ... Feb-May, 12", flower with shiny yellow petals
Bush Monkeyflower ... Mar-Aug, 3', yellow flower, sticky leaves
Calypso Orchid ... Mar-Apr, 6-8", single pink flower, leafless stem
Checkerbloom ... Mar-May, 12", pink 1" flower, lobed leaves
Cream Cups ... Mar-May, 8", creamy yellow 1 inch flowers
Crimson Clover ... Apr-June, 12", bright red 1" flower, non-native
Chinese Houses ... Apr-May, 10", pink and white flowers in tiers
Clarkia ... May-Aug, 10", bright pink flower, blooms late
Clintonia ... Apr-June, 18", shiny leaves, pink flower clusters
Columbine ... Apr-June, 18", flowers nodding, red and yellow
Douglas Iris ... Mar-May, 12", purple 2 inch flower
Fairy Bells ... Feb-July, 2', greenish white, bell-shaped flowers
False Lupine ... Mar-May, 2', yellow pea flower, 3 leaflets
Farewell to Spring ... Apr-June, 8-16", dark pink flowers
Fiddleneck ... Mar-June, 12", orange flowers coiled at end of stem
Filaree ... Mar-Aug, 4", pink-lavender flower, grassy hillsides
Footsteps of Spring ... Jan-May, 4", low growing, yellow flower
Forget-me-not ... Feb-June, 12", light blue flowers, non-native
Gold Fields ... Mar-June, 8", small yellow daisy-like flower
Hound's Tongue ... Feb-Apr, 2', large leaves, blue flowers
Indian Paintbrush ... Mar-June, 12", red-orange flower
Indian Warrior ... Jan-Apr, 10", fern-like leaves, red flowers
Larkspur ... Apr-May, 18", blue 1 inch flower with spur
Lupine ... Mar-May, 12", divided leaves, blue pea flower
Milkmaids ... Jan-Mar, 16", most common white flower plant
Mission Bells ... Jan-Mar, 18", purple bell-shaped flower
Modesty ... Mar-May, 8", trailing plant, 1/8 inch white flowers
Morning Glory ... Mar-Sept, 2', twining vine, pinkish-white flowers
Mules Ears ... Mar-June, 18", large leaves, yellow sunflower
Oakland Star Tulip... May-June, 6", white flower, basal leaf
Pitcher Sage ... Aromatic shrub 3' high, bell-shaped white flower
Popcorn Flower ... Apr-May, 12", small white flowers
Poppy, California ... Mar-Oct, 12", yellow cup-shaped flower
Red Larkspur ... Mar-June, 18", red 1 inch flower with spur
Redwood Sorrel ... Mar-June, 6", pink flowers, clover-like leaves
Sanicle ... Mar-June, 12", yellow or purple flower balls, lobed leaves
Shooting Star ... Feb-Apr, 12", pink petals turned back
False Solomon's Seal ... Feb-Apr, 12", bright green leaves, white flower
Slink Pod ... Jan-Feb, 4", broad spotted leaves, purple flower

111

Star Flower ... Mar-July, 8", whorl of leaves, pink flowers
Sun Cup ... Feb-May, 5", basal leaves, yellow cupped flower
Tarweed ... July-Nov, 18-30", yellow composite flower, aromatic, sticky stem
Trillium ... Feb-Mar, 12", leaves and petals in sets of three
Woodland Star ... Mar-May, 16", small white star-like flower
Wood Rose ... Shrub 3' high with prickles, small 1" pink flowers
Yarrow ... Apr-Sept, 18", fern-like leaves, white flower cluster
Yellow Mariposa Lily .. May-June, 14", flower with 3 yellow petals
Zigadene ... Feb-Apr, 16", robust plant with white flowers

Index of Shrubs and Trees

Bay ... Tree to 100' tall, dark green aromatic leaves
Big-Leaf Maple ... Deciduous tree 15-90' tall, deeply lobed leaves
Black Oak, California ... Deciduous tree 30-75' , deeply lobed leaves
Broom ... Non-native invasive shrub to 9', yellow pea flowers in spring
Buckeye ... Deciduous tree or shrub, fragrant flowers in May and June
Canyon Live Oak ... (or Goldcup Oak) to 60', leaves grey to gold beneath
Ceanothus ... Shrub to 15', spring flowers in clusters
Chamise ... Shrub 3-10' high, needle-like leaves
Chaparral Oak ... Shrub 3-10', oval leaf, edge smooth or serrated
Chaparral Pea ... Spiny shrub 2-6', bright pink pea flowers
Chinquapin ... Shrub or tree 6-60' tall, leaves green above, gold below
Coast Live Oak ... Tree 30-75', oval cup-shaped leaves
Coffeeberry ... Rounded shrub 3-12' tall, ripe berries black or red
Coulter Pine ... Tree 50-75', large cones, needles in bunches of 3
Coyote Brush ... Shrub of coastal scrub 3-12' high, toothed leaves
Douglas Fir ... Tree to 250' tall, flat 1" needles, 2-3" cones
Elk Clover ... Deciduous shrub to 4', very large leaves, moist areas
Hazel,California ... Deciduous shrub 6-18' , leaves softly hairy
Huckleberry ... Shrub 3-8' tall, oval shiny leaves, edible fruit in fall
Leather Oak ... Shrub 3-9', small oval leaves with spiny teeth
Manzanita ... Shrub with reddish-brown bark, urn-shaped white flower
Madrone ... Tree 15-120' tall, smooth red bark, shiny leaves
Nutmeg, California ... Tree 15-90' tall, stiff pointed needles, fruit 2"
Ocean Spray ... Shrub 4-18' tall, oval leaves toothed, white flower
Poison Oak ... Shrub to 9', 3 leaflets, small white flower clusters, climbing
Red Alder ... Deciduous tree 45-75' along stream banks, oval leaf
Redwood ... Tree to 260', branches forming flat sprays, 1" cones
Sargent Cypress ... Tree of serpentine 10-45' , leaves scale-like
Scrub Oak ... Shrub 3-9', oval leaves, shiny above, pale beneath, rare
Silk Tassel Bush ... Shrub to 20', oval leaves, wavy edge, long catkins
Tanoak ... Tree 10-120' with conical crown, veined leaves
Tree Poppy ... Shrub 3-9', leaves gray green, 4 yellow petals in spring
Toyon ... Shrub 6-30' high, toothed leaves, red summer berries
Western Azalea ... Deciduous shrub to 9', fragrant flowers in June
Yerba Santa ... Aromatic shrub 3' tall, dark green leaves, white flower

All trees and shrubs are evergreen unless described as deciduous.

A18 Local Resources

There are a variety of public and private organizations providing resources for Mt Tamalpais. All phone numbers are in the 415 area.

Marin Municipal Water District

The Marin Municipal Water District occupies the largest area on Mt Tamalpais. It includes almost all of the north side of the mountain plus a large area from West Point Inn to the Mtn Home Inn.

Sky Oaks Ranger Station 459-5267

Mt Tamalpais State Park

Mt Tamalpais State Park is the second largest area covered by this book. The park occupies most of the area on the south side of the mountain excluding Muir Woods and the area around West Point Inn.

Pantoll Ranger Station and Campground 388-2070
East Peak Visitor Center - Hours 10-4 on weekends
Steep Ravine Cabins and Campground - Mistix 1-800-444-7275

National Park Service

Both Muir Woods and GGNRA are administered by the National Park Service. All of Muir Woods is included in this book. Very little GGNRA.

Golden Gate National Recreation Area 556-0560
Muir Woods National Monument 388-2595
Golden Gate National Park Association - 556-2236

Marin County Open Space District

The County Open Space District oversees dozens of areas in Marin, but just Blithedale Ridge Open Space is included in this book.

Marin County Open Space District Office 499-6387

Related organizations include:

Mt Tam Interpretative Association - PO Box 3318, San Rafael 94912
Mountain Play Association - Plays in May and June, 383-0155
Sierra Club - Weekly hikes, 6014 College, Oakland 94618
Tamalpa Runners - PO Box 701, Corte Madera 94925
Tamalpais Conservation Club - 870 Market St, Room 562, SF 94102
Mt Tamalpais History Project - c/o Mill Valley Public Library
Bike Trails Council of Marin - PO Box 494, Fairfax 94978
California Native Plant Society - 1 Harrison Ave, Sausalito 94965

A19 Bibliography

Aker, R. *Sir Francis Drake at Drakes Bay*. Drakes Navigator
Guild, 1978.
Bakker, E.S. *An Island Called California*. University of California
Press, 1971.
Bowen, O.E., Jr. *Rocks and Minerals of the San Francisco Bay
Region*. University of California Press, 1966.
Brockman, C. F. *Trees of North America*. Golden Press, 1968.
Erickson's *Mount Tamalpais Trail Map*. Eureka Cartography, 1991.
Fairley, Lincoln. *Mount Tamalpais: A History*. Scottwall
Associates, 1987
Gilliam, H. *Weather of the San Francisco Bay Region*. University of
California Press, 1962.
Gudde, E.G. *California Place Names*. University of California
Press, 1969.
Hickman, J.C., Ed. *The Jepson Manual*. University of California
Press, 1993 .
Howell, J.T. *Marin Flora*. University of California Press, 1970.
Kruckeberg, A.R. *California Serpentines*. University of California
Press, 1984.
Mason, J. *The Making of Marin*. North Shore Books, 1975.
McHoul, L. *Wildflowers Of Marin*. The Tamal Land Press, 1979.
Miller, G. Tyler. *Living in the Environment*, Fifth ed., Wadsworth
Publishing Co., 1988.
Morrato, M.J. *California Archaeology*. Academic Press, 1984.
Munz, P.A. *A California Flora*. University of California Press, 1959.
Niehaus, T.F. & Ripper, C.L. *A Field Guide to Pacific Wildflowers*.
Houghton Mifflin, 1976.
Olmsted & Bros Map Co. *Trails of Mt. Tamalpais and the Marin
Headlands*. 5th edition.
Olson, R. *The History of Mount Tamalpais*. A thesis presented to the
faculty of the Consortium of the California State University, 1985.
Spitz, Barry. *Tamalpais Trails*. Potrero Meadow Publishing Co, 1990.
Teather, L. *Place Names of Marin*. Scottwall Associates, 1986.
Whitnah, D.L. *An Outdoor Guide to the San Francisco Bay Area*.
Wilderness Press, 1976.
Wurm, Theodore G. and Graves, Alvin C. *The Crookedest Railroad In
The World*. 2nd Edition. Howell-North Books, 1960.
Handbook of North American Indians. Vol. 8, Smithsonian
Institute, 1978.
Environmental Planning Study. Marin Muncipal Water
District, 1976.

About the authors

Kay Martin has a Masters degree in botany from San Francisco State University and works as a volunteer docent for Bay Shore Studies. She is active with the California Native Plant Society and is a member of the Tamalpa Runners. In training for five marathons, she has logged several thousand miles running the trails of Mt Tamalpais.

Don Martin teaches physics and computer science at the College of Marin. He has co-authored four computer books, all published by Howard W. Sams, and a study guide, *How to be a Successful Student*.

The Martins have also written and published the book, *Point Reyes National Seashore*. They are members of the Sierra Club, Nature Conservancy and Audubon Society. They have four grown children.

Bob Johnson is a well-known Marin County illustrator and designer. He has illustrated over thirty plant books, twenty computer books and a variety of other books, posters and artwork.

Order Form

Point Reyes National Seashore
A Hiking and Nature Guide
by Don and Kay Martin
1992

Here is the best and most complete guide book to Point Reyes National Seashore. It describes 34 round-trip hikes on Point Reyes and includes over 80 illustrations of plants, tidepool critters, birds and animals. Each hike includes a 3-D map like the Mt Tam book. The price is $9.95 plus tax and shipping.

Books may be ordered from your local bookstore or directly from the publisher at the address below.

Martin Press
P.O. Box 2109
San Anselmo, CA 94979

The price for direct ordering from the publisher is:

1-3 copies at $9.95 each.
3 or more copies at $8.95 each.

Please include $2.50 per order to cover shipping and tax.